KIDS OF KING

KIDS OF KING

Faith, Family, and Love
will see you through it all!

By
Naomi J. Kinney

XULON PRESS

Xulon Press
2301 Lucien Way #415
Maitland, FL 32751
407.339.4217
www.xulonpress.com

Unless otherwise indicated, Scripture quotations taken from the King James Version (KJV) – *public domain*.

Paperback ISBN-13: 978-1-6628-3703-6
Ebook ISBN-13: 978-1-6628-3704-3

For my awesome parents, my dear siblings,
and for my precious daughter Julia

Table of Contents

A light-hearted, melodious glance at a Black Midwest orphan girl's personal odyssey through tragedy, grief, spurring challenging questions about her racially-charged history (along with her 8 older siblings) – the startling account of how, through introspection and spiritual awakening, a "mess" pushed her to find her mission in life.

Introduction

In America, an average of 132 people per day take their own lives. According to the American Foundation for Suicide Prevention, suicide death is the 10th leading cause of death in our country, 47,511 people committed suicide in 2019, and 1.38 million people attempted suicide in the same year. If you're a person who, like me, is a survivor of a suicide death in your family, then this book (I hope) might be a helpful inspiration for you to show you that every situation is surmountable with God and a loving, supportive network around you – if you tap into it. This is our story. Although funny at times, it is one of compounded loss shared by my "clan", told from my perspective as the youngest of the nine. It is both an autobiography and a testimonial on how faith helped me (us) overcome my (our) loss(es). Raised as Black Catholics while living in a predominantly white conservative Midwest city (Cincinnati, Ohio), my 8 siblings and I have overcome some very tough challenges (to say the least), and this is the story of our survival as we grew up on the banks of the Ohio River during the 50s -80s particularly. This is also a "study" of sorts (for me) of my parents and a look back at their lives and what prompted them to generate "the Kids of King" (me and my 8 siblings). It is a particularly close look back at my father's life and how his tragic death rocked our innocence and has lingering effects for each of us uniquely. There are many flashbacks of stories about the life and times of the Kinney family on Grantwood Avenue and attending St. Mark Catholic Church and School in the Evanston community of Cincinnati. It showcases how tragedy can occur within any family such as our big close-knit, faithful bunch; we are just an example. Additionally, it is a story that explores how mental illness was/is prominent particularly in the African-American community, what societal factors influence that, and how it can affect any good family of color (sometimes prompted or nurtured by their external circumstances). My message is to encourage that we all continue to check on one another, those within our circle and those beyond, like never before. Even "the strong ones" need attention and love, especially in these difficult times, as I am writing this book amidst the infamous "COVID-19 Global Pandemic" (2020-2021) and amidst all the racial, civil, and political strife that unfortunately continues in our country. Additionally, May is Mental Health Month and September is Suicide Prevention Month, but we need to check on one another on both fronts year-round. Just recently in 2021, former NCAA track champion and son of former Olympic Gold medalist Cameron Burrell sadly took his own young, promising life. "We many never know why Cameron made such a decision, his dad, Leroy Burrell, stated to the Associated Press. "We encourage anyone who *may be struggling in their lives to reach out for help. You are not alone, and you are surrounded by more people who love and care for you than you may think in a dark moment." Cameron was the NCAA 100-meter champion for Houston in 2018, and anchored the Cougars' 4x100 championship relay team that year.*

One in the same, there are many that return from military life, and cannot handle the post-traumatic stress disorder (PTSD) that wracks their brain. Many of these brave men and women die in silence without support, but we must do better at keeping an eye on one another and detect the symptoms.... I share them here, and how to respond.

Note: *If you or someone you know is in crisis, PLEASE call the toll-free National Suicide Prevention Lifeline at 1-800-273-TALK (8255), available 24 hours a day, 7 days a week. The service is available to anyone. All calls are confidential.*

http://www.suicidepreventionlifeline.org

*The story of loss in this book also shows how we **all** have a cross to bear in life, but have the ability to manage that and change that "burden" into a blessing. So, this is indeed a story of promise and hope of making something good and meaningful out of such negative circumstances. I know that many, particularly in the Black community and especially in this day and time, can really relate to the pressures of oppression and prejudice regardless of their location in this country that affect many mentally, physically, and spiritually. My father particularly (as I myself also* *learned) has experienced a full range of emotions while navigating the "pressures" and insanity of racism, many in our hometown but this is rampant in many cities across the U.S... the results have been devastating for anyone who is the victim. My book is primarily a call for **unity** of the black and white communities to come together, knowing the harsh affects and outcomes if we fail to do so as a country, as a society, as a global community. We miss out on the opportunity to love one another and be more productive together, making our country live up to its creed and be the great nation it really is. I'm not expecting utopia, but I think we can get very close with more love and direct caring for one another, even the local stranger. Instead of hating one another, we should <u>learn</u> more about one another and **self-analyze** why we hate others unlike ourselves as we do. We should **respect** one another more, and we should definitely **educate** ourselves on one another (our cultures, religions, practices, etc.) to break down the fear we have of one another, those who are different from ourselves. There is room enough and plenty of resources on this earth for ALL of us to share – **we are ALL children of God**. As our planet gets smaller and smaller, we should all continue on this earth with the spiritual mission of brotherhood, multiculturalism, unity, and inclusion.*

Finally, I wrote this book also to highlight a bit of an amazing, legendary music business ran right in our own Evanston community: the history of THE legendary King Records in Cincinnati, Ohio, which ironically was located only two blocks away from the house in which we all were raised. It was also where my father found some solace and expression through singing. King Records was actually the little-known origin of much musical talent coming out of Ohio. Besides the Cincinnati chili (Skyline preferably... you must eat some if you ever pass through this town!), King Records is the best kept secret not just in Evanston, but in Ohio! So, read on, and enjoy the story of "The Kids of King".

Acknowledgements:

This group of people are the "angels' mentioned in this story:

My parents: Robert Lee "Buddy" Kinney, Sr. and Alfreda "Sissy" Robinson Kinney

All Eight of My Dear Siblings: Carl Vincent Kinney, Cynthia Elaine Kinney Smith, Cecilia Ann Kinney Yancey, Angela Jewel Kinney, Francis Wayne Kinney, Alfred "Chico" Kinney, Karen Marie Kinney Malek Bouquet, and Robert Lee "Bobby" Kinney, Jr. *(the latter is now deceased - RIP)*

- All my Robinson aunts and uncles *(Especially Naomi Robinson Frazier -* ***"Aunt Chick"*** *and Uncles Gus, Alfred "Sonny", and Raymond "Ray")*
- All my Kinney aunts and uncles *(Especially Aunts Mable, Shirley, and Mary along with Uncles Sherman, George, and Frank Kinney)*
- **Fr. Dennis "Denny" Kinderman** *(Rector of St. Mark Catholic Church in Evanston)*
- **Sr. Rose Helene Wildehaus** *(Principal of St. Mark Catholic Elementary School in Evanston – She died in August 2021 just before she could read my*

manuscript, but I was blessed to visit her in Dayton, OH in 2020 and tell her all she meant to me and my family. May she rest in heavenly peace.)

- **Mr. and Mrs. William James Madison III** *(My mentors − Brenda Madison taught at St. Mark School; I can't say enough about how these folks who "held me over", constantly inspiring me.)*

Other acknowledgements:

I also want to thank my best friends through grade school (Deneen Robinson), through high school (Deneen, Monica Berry - RIP, and Tammy Jones Andersson), and through college and into adulthood (Sabrina Coleman Thomas) for holding my hand and getting me through every difficult moment in my life. I love each of you like sisters. I also must thank the first people who read my rough manuscript and gave me lots of advice on the particulars of how to write this story: Again, Sabrina Thomas was one of the first to read it. My long-time friend Jeffrey Allen also from the Midwest (East St. Louis, IL). And finally, my former co-worker, my "spec" and soror Ingrid Williams (of THE Delta Sigma Theta Sorority, Incorporated of THE Federal City Alumnae Chapter in Washington, D.C.). Also thank you to soror Terri Ann Johnson, also an FCAC soror and author who told me "Just start writing!" Each of you all kept encouraging me when I did not even see the end of the tunnel on this project, and for this I am immensely grateful! I love all my sorors immensely!!

I also want to thank Wanda Childs (another author) for providing me formal training on the process of self-publishing and moving my further toward my goals of this publication (and for sharing your resources). Without your guidance, candid feedback, and inspiration to start and to continue writing, I would not have this body of work. Thank you to everyone who shared stories and the history of Evanston, Cincinnati, and the Kinney family especially Alex "Buddy" Jackson. And to every other person I did not mention here, charge it to my head and not my heart that I missed acknowledging you here. You ALL have inspired me along my path in life; I thank you also, because it got me to this place.... I am ever grateful.

Thank you, to all of my loving teachers who guided me like I was their child: to Mrs. Rosa Moore (RIP), Mrs. Pat Burke, Mr. Ron Czerbak, Mrs. Joyce Smith, Mr. Duane Drotar, all the nuns of the Precious Blood (and all the staff at St. Mark Catholic Elementary School); to all the staff at Ursuline Academy of Cincinnati in Blue Ash - to Mrs. Ruthanne Palmer, Sr. Joan Roach, Sr. MaryAnn Jensen, Sr. Peter, Sr. Regina Winters; to all the staff at Central State University in Wilberforce, Ohio - Dr. Terence Glass, head of the English Department (who directly taught me about writing), Dr. William Felker, head of the Foreign Language Department (inspired me much later in life to write this book), and Mrs. Audrey Norman (former Sociology professor and Director of Alumni Affairs – RIP) for always inspiring me toward excellence and being the best I could be in life. I thank every "teacher" and "angel" that has crossed my path in life (and those that have yet to cross my path). My teachers each showed me the possibilities in my life and to believe in and expect miracles from my faith, diligence, and intent to stay strong in spite of my challenges. They also have shown me the importance of caring for and sharing your knowledge with others regardless of race, language, creed, and lifestyle, and history. Teachers make our world a kinder, more constructive, and more productive one (as opposed to all the prejudice, conflict, and apathy that brings about our destruction). I want use my God-given talents to be more like them: to be God's vessel of handiwork and be impactful in someone's life, giving God all the glory. I can't change the world (God will do that), but I can do my part for humanity through His power and grace.

I pay tribute to everyone in "my village", but most importantly, I give thanks to my Lord and Savior Jesus Christ). All have taught me, guided me, carried me through, and helped me experience nothing but "a wonderful life".

Note: *All biblical quotations are taken from the King James version of the Bible.*

Chapter 1:

Reflecting on My Past

T here comes a time in your life (and after such a tragic life early on) when you look back and wonder, **"What really happened in my past? How did things really transpire? Was it like I was told as a young girl, or was I shielded to protect my innocence when so many strange things were occurring?"** When you begin to analyze all that has transpired in your life, and you analyze whether or not you had a good upbringing, you begin to make connections to your adult life. This is where I am, really always am, self-evaluating and wondering why (and how) I am who I am. This book is about self-exploration and introspection about my origin. It is a journey through my personal history, the history of *my* Cincinnati, Ohio, how my family and I experienced our community, our city and the history of our (Black) people there. As I have been in life evaluation mode on this journey, I am reflecting on what really happened and to evaluate the origin and current placement of my emotions, character, and personality. I definitely ran into some revelations, some great points of interest that are part of *my* Cincinnati and family history, and I also ran into my own sentiments along the way. But this has been cleansing and a revelation; for that I am truly thankful and blessed.

> *"I the Lord search the heart and examine the mind, to reward each person according to their conduct, according to what their deeds deserve. Seek the Lord with all your heart and He will be found by you." –* **Jeremiah 17:10**

> *"And ye shall seek me, and find me, when ye shall search for me with all your heart."* **– Jeremiah 29:13-14**

Particularly during my time after college, I realized that there were several gaps in my memory of being a child growing up in Evanston. I had/have so many questions about me, my siblings, and my parents. **How did *I* happen to be the baby of nine children? Did my siblings adore me (as I remembered), did they see me as just another "crumb snatcher" in the clan, or was I just another burden to my parents? What did my parents experience while growing up in Cincinnati?** I never really got the chance until later in life to ask them how they handled all the challenges that we all experienced growing up. **What were my parents really like as a young loving couple with so many children? What did they experience in the community and in Cincinnati during the time we were growing up? And what happened to their relationship to make things occur as they did?** Now, with a child of my own, these are just some of the questions that I have been wanting to share the answers to with her. I wrote this book to try to answer some of those questions and to come to closure with the events that have occurred early in my life while I was so young, and not yet ready to really understand their profundity. I now have a much greater understanding of life and why some of those things did happen, but still naturally question why. I have learned a lot of hard lessons from my (our) life's history and tragedy, and now I am sharing them with you so that you might learn to treasure *your* family's history too, however eventful or "colorful" that past may be. I also share my (our) story to help other families in crisis or who have similar tragic experiences to let them know that with faith and family all things are truly surmountable, although in the moment it doesn't always feel so.

One thing that I do know is that the family that I have been born into is absolutely amazing, and you will find that out in this text. I *knew* growing up that "the Kinney family" was special, but as I grew and as we all persevered through all of our personal and mutual challenges, it was obvious that we were (and are) indeed a *very* special family... me and my eight siblings, "the Kinney clan" as we were referred to in the Evanston community of Cincinnati, Ohio... big enough to be a baseball team. We are now a family that many look up to because of our steadfastness through the struggle, our strength, our unity, and the deep love, support, respect we have for each other. Not only this, but we know how to support others in our family and community...

we understand the significance and the impact of that on people's lives. This is where my/our story begins, but not how it ends, for we continue to be blessed and to bless others in our circle. Learn from and cherish our experiences, as many families have gone through a lot of what we have, but know that for every challenging situation you may face **God is able** and "this, too, shall pass". We surely stay ever-grateful for God's grasp on our lives...

But making beautiful endings out of impossible situations is God's specialty. He never wastes a single trial. He transforms it all for our good and His Holy Glory. If we keep following the light of God's presence through this dark and difficult world, we all will see God turn around our impossible messes... that's His promise! Nothing can stop the amazing redemptive power of our God. It's amazing what God will do with a broken life if you give Him all the pieces.

> *"Fear not, for I am with you; be not dismayed for I am your God; I will strengthen you. I will help you, I will uphold you with my righteous hand."*
> **— Isaiah 41:10**

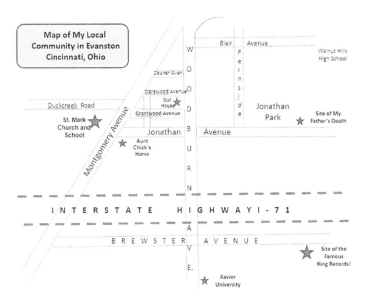

Map of My Local Community in Evanston Cincinnati, Ohio

Evanston Families on Grantwood:

- Mr. Orlando
- The Kinneys
- The Browns
- The Bradshaws
- Mr. Johnson
- The Cooks
- Mr. Gardner
- The Robinsons
- Mr. Curtis (Elisha)
- The Burstons
- The Jacksons (both Jackson families)
- The Howells
- The Berrys
- Mr. White
- The Warners/Travis

Chapter 2:

An Epiphany

"In those days there was no king in Israel; every
man did that which was right in his own eyes."
– Judges 21: 25

*E*veryone (at least I hope) says to themselves at some
point in their lives, "Someday, I'm gonna figure out
where I really come from, and why I am who I am." It can
be cathartic, enlightening, but also heart-breaking and
disappointing. Yet and still, it can be cleansing, healing,
and necessary. While I have been doing all this thinking
on my family's history, I have been documenting some
facts and exploring some of the characters and events
that have occurred. Especially now, prompted by so much
that is occurring within the Black community and our
country now, I feel the need to personally explore and
examine how many of these same issues have impacted
me and my family historically and this makes us what we
are today. For, I was born in 1963, a very turbulent time
in our country for civil rights, but why does it still feel like
we're still in 1963 in many ways. How is it that nothing

has changed in 58 years in this country, those same issues that so adversely affect the communities of all persons of color in this country? As I look back, although I'm full of disappointment at our country, my "epiphany" has been catalytic and has prompted me to action in my life with the guidance of the Holy Spirit.

Today feels like a good day, taking in the sunshine here on my back deck, reading Scripture, drinking my daily dose of soothing green tea, listening to a peaceful meditation audio from my inspirational mentee and friend, LaShone, and allowing the sun to bathe into my skin permitting all the vitamin D that I badly need during this recent pandemic that has spread across the globe. Unfortunately, the thank you cards I used to buy in bulk are now replaced with bulk purchases of sympathy cards instead in order to accommodate and comfort all the people/families near me experiencing loss now due to COVID-19. Over a half million people have died of this awful virus already (numbers still rising), and under continuous quarantine I'm praying hard as I do every morning like now (especially since this pandemic hit us in the U.S. in early 2020). I'm praying for the comfort of those who have lost a loved one, healing for those stricken with the virus now, and praying that me and my family avoid its deadly path as it makes its way across the U.S. and the world. Having been taught in my youth to pray early in the morning, this is the precious hour that I have for daily introspection, to give thanks for every day that I am given (whether sunny or not), and then I begin planning tasks for the day like always. It helps me organize my thoughts for the day, think of others in needs, and rejuvenate myself physically, mentally, and spiritually.

On this day particularly, I woke up with a feeling of happiness and hope now that the U.S. Presidential election is over, and a new President (Joseph Biden) would soon be sworn in along with a history-making Black/Asian female Vice President (Kamala Harris). Members of the U.S. House of Representatives were about to ratify the election process officially today on Capitol Hill in Washington, DC on January 6th, 2021. Additionally, many (not only African-Americans) were hyped to celebrate the double win of Senate seats in Georgia by Jon Ossoff and Rev. Raphael Warnock turning that state Democratic (Blue) for the first time in history. It was to be a celebratory day for the Democratic Party in the U.S., and a feeling of elation and liberation was sweeping across the country. At least we thought...

Yet this day I also had a sense of dread deep down inside from this series of recent seemingly fortunate events for our country, knowing that many in this country were/are *not* happy about the 2020 election outcomes. I felt like something bad was about to happen. Something told me that they would want to make a statement expressing that negative frustration – in the worst way. It was the same dread I felt when President Barack Obama was elected for the first (and second) time (and especially when he and his beautiful First Lady Michelle Obama stepped out of the limousine during their Inauguration parade in DC) – that someone would want to shatter that dream that many of us had of finally having a Black President (and First Lady) in this country. It's not like there are not qualified men and women of color out there (for this and many high-level positions in this country). They've just never had the opportunity and never before had the ability to fight so hard for the change. So, this indeed should have been a time to celebrate, yet in that moment it was similar to the "Obama walk in the Inaugural parade" that we feared something bad might happen.

After coming inside the house from the deck and making my traditional morning green tea, I cut on the television to check the news as I always do. Sometimes I pause in doing so, until I'm ready to brace for the day, but today, again, I expected nothing but a celebration of positivity! The morning news is often part of the morning routine of many who live in the "DMV" (DC, MD, and VA area), so many like myself would normally be tuned in right about then. Many in the DC area would also definitely be tuned in just like me. However, as I watched what was progressing on the television in front of me, I could hear instead of a celebration there was a low-volume version of Billie Holliday's song in the air - "Strange Fruit"... it was surreal.

I'm watching and searching the screen for what should be a celebration for a history-making election win – instead... out of nowhere news commentators cut normal programming and go to a livestream video at the U.S. Capitol Building in Washington, DC. I now see on my tv screen, not a celebration of a new American President; instead I see a fast-moving angry mob with confederate flags storming the Capitol Building in DC... absolutely unprecedented! **What the heck is going on here? When and where did this commotion get started? What prompted this?!?!** We all later would find out what (and who) did prompt all this uproar, and to this day unfortunately there still is no accountability for what occurred that day: the lives lost and the injuries sustained, the physical destruction and vandalism to the historic Capitol Building and property, and the risk of an overthrow of our precious democracy and government as we know it... an unprecedented lack of accountability... and we all know the impetus behind all this.

Later all the rationalizations of what occurred made me even angrier. (I'm still hearing "Strange Fruit" narrating in my brain as I'm thinking through this whole scenario.) This really is just history simply repeating itself in an unprecedented show of white privilege and supremacy on full display for the whole world to see. America's dirty laundry was definitely hanging out on January 6, 2021. It not only made me angry that this was permitted to happen, but it made me angrier that things would go on like normal for many thereafter, like nothing ever happened on that infamous day. It made me start thinking more about the many injustices me and my family have suffered in the past. My childhood seemed very idyllic (for the most part), but some of this prompted my thoughts about things growing up that were not so idyllic for me and my family. I know that my family and community tried to shield me from some of that ugly prejudice growing up when they could, but definitely not all of it... some of it we had to experience for ourselves to really understand the gravity of it and how it made us feel. Some "incidents" occurred a long time ago and some in the recent past, and now this "incident" is occurring today right before my eyes again! How is it that things are still the same to this day with no real changes having occurred in race relations in this country, although many have protested and protested about equal rights? **Is there no one with a soul listening or seeing this?**

As I self-evaluate more, I began to re-examine the ways this has stained our American society, it is our flaw (and could be our downfall). It has negatively affected many in the Black community, and it surely affected me and my family historically as well. And this made me very angry and dis-appointed at America. Today I don't like my country. Today I'm not necessarily proud to say that I am an American, not seeing this before me. Although I would always have hoped that this would change for America and thinking that I could even make an impact on that happening in my life (being bilingual speaking/teaching Spanish and being a long-time instructor of Cultural Diversity, Equity, & Inclusion). My class participants would continually tell me stories about how the ugly monster of prejudice continues to appear in our country even to the hopeful and even when we least expect it (sometimes when we *do* expect it, kind of like how I was feeling on the morning of January 6, 2021). I was indeed feeling very hopeful at first, and prej-udice and white supremacy surely popped my balloon of hope on that day (as it has often squashed the perceptions of hope held by many persons of color in the past).

The emotions I felt while watching the storming of the Capitol Building in DC January 6, 2021 got me thinking even harder about my family's history, upbringing, and life as an adult living in very conservative Cincinnati, Ohio – where there have been many well-known race riots (from 1829 to 2020). Why does this keep happening over and over again in our country? And why does it keep happening in my hometown, even so recently? First, let me explain a bit about Cincinnati, Ohio historically and the environment in which I was raised....

"The Queen City" is located right on the Mason-Dixon line (the Ohio River), and is a historic spot where many Blacks escaping the perils of slavery risked their lives trying to cross that river from Kentucky into Cincinnati, Ohio and onto freedom of the Union (leaving behind the Confederacy of the south), also captured so gruesomely in Toni Morrison's novel "Beloved" (Knopf Publications, 1987). The Ohio river flows from Cairo, Illinois where it spills into the Mississippi River, and its eastern portion ends in Pittsburgh, Pennsylvania where the "three rivers" meet: the Ohio, the Monongahela, and the Allegheny (where Pittsburgh gets the name for Three River Stadium being located only blocks from the convergence of these three waterways there). Ohio got its English name from the Native Americans (Iroquois) who called it "O-Y-O" which means "great river", and there is much Native American history and relics across the state to remind us of that. But besides learning about Fort Ancient in Lebanon, Ohio (precious Native American burial ground shaped like a serpent), we did not learn a lot about their history while growing up in Ohio. And we only really learned about Black History during February (and even that information did not highlight our many accomplishments in this country!). But I now realize who designed that curriculum, and it was not people of color. Although it wasn't common knowledge, Cincinnati historically, really *was* a place of many cultures coming together, but one group always stayed in control.

In the early 1830s and 1840s, Irish and German families emigrated to Ohio fleeing political persecution and famine, and many of them found work in the meat-packing, construction, railroad, and other industries, making Cincinnati eventually become more populous and prosperous. It was called "Over the Rhine" by the Germans, because the view of the river over into Kentucky reminded many of them of the Rhine river that flows through Germany. Cincinnati historically has always been considered a place of great commerce, being a port for boats going east to west to stop and get their "fun": sex, drugs, alcohol, food, and they could stock goods for the long trip ahead east or west. Similar to current day, everyone in the region then (Kentucky, Indiana, Pennsylvania) would often make their way through Cincinnati, Ohio for some "big city fun" at some point in their lives, and the Ohio river was the center of it all.

My "Aunt Chick" would take us to the Public Landing on the waterfront, where people could launch their boats and we would innertube and dip in the river during the summers to keep cool. I recall once her staring into the river sadly saying "the souls of many of our people are at the bottom of that river, namesake", and then she sighed. She then told me how runaway slaves would often try to cross during the winter while the river was frozen, but did not always make it across to freedom. Some fell through what they thought was ice and drowned in the Ohio river. I then realized how much desperation it must have taken to make a move like that. Life must have been pretty bad as a slave in Kentucky (probably worse the further south you went). I then began to look across the river at Kentucky and a fear grew in me of what was over there. But that's just what prejudice is: fear. Only now do I recognize the real point of origin of that emotion that welled in me that day listening to my aunt tell that harrowing tale.

Our family has a touch of the Irish heritage in our blood through my father's side of our family, the Kinneys. And ironically, much of the city's racial strife has been between the police (many of whom have Irish heritage) and the African-American community. However, it's ironic that although many policemen and women in the US are Irish, historically the Irish community has been viewed as the "trouble-makers" in the immigrant community in the US. The flood of the Irish into law enforcement in the 2nd half of the 19th century was particularly striking, because just a couple of decades earlier city authorities had viewed Irish immigrants as the source of serious crime problems and overall organized crime. In fact, many northern U.S. cities invented their police departments as a way to control the "Irish problem" After the great potato crop famine in Ireland in the 1840s, families fled to America with no money and ended up living in shantytown and slum city segments of New York, Philadelphia, and Boston (and Cincinnati was also one of those towns where the Irish immigrant community pocketed itself in the U.S., trying to find a "better life"). They took whatever jobs they could get as skilled laborers and domestic servants, making very little money and squashing out those minor job opportunities for the already limited African-American community in America (as they are white and more acceptable to those providing opportunities at that time in our country's history). And like other struggling groups coming to America with limited opportunities, they turned to petty theft or sex work to make ends meet. And thereby prospered in the "dangerous and busy river life" on the Ohio river in Cincinnati in the early 20th century like many immigrant communities, but many still struggled to survive right alongside the Black community, who fared far worse than any other ethnic group there. Unfortunately, that still continues to this day.

Irish immigrants were not only feared because they were used to a rougher way of life back in Ireland, one that included lots of alcohol drinking and frequent clashes between rival clans in their community. Americans had a lot of prejudice against the Irish community for its rough, combative history, but mostly for its religion: Catholicism.

Another reason for the great migration of Irish to the U.S. was the battle between Protestantism and Catholicism that still goes on in Ireland to this day, and has often led to deadly results there over time. Many of those religious prejudices still transfer to today, and it has been evident over time in Cincinnati as well. There are many Protestant churches in Cincinnati, but there are SO many more Catholic parishes across Cincinnati that flourished especially from 1940s-1970s, like our St. Mark Catholic church and school in Evanston. In the 70s and 80s many issues arose with priests (many of them also Irish) forced into being celibate and, in turn, many were accused and convicted of sexual molestation of minors within their parish communities. This led to many of my fellow-Catholics (in Cincinnati and across the nation) to leave the Catholic church, file law suits against the various churches and Archdioceses, and forced the shut-down of some Catholic churches and schools across the city (and country). This is exactly why (after a long, hard fight of our Evanston community members), our dear St. Mark church and school had to eventually be closed. *(St. Mark School is now called Alliance Public Charter School of Cincinnati, property purchased by National Heritage Academies. The Evanston community (and the children there) benefitted greatly from that acquisition. The Evanston Community Council is currently fighting the battle to keep the church open and repurposed as a community recreation/meeting center, since Evanston is now going through a major gentrification.)*

Besides Catholic prejudices against the Irish (in Cincinnati and across the country), the Irish community over time was still held to many religious and cultural prejudices, but instead tried to redeem itself in image by becoming part of the "law and order" of the community and many of the men joined the ranks of the police department in their local cities (like Cincinnati) to counter the "drunken and disorderly" image. In joining law enforcement in the late 19th century, this community found a way to gain some positive traction in America. But as law enforcement, they would also *control* a lot of what went on across the city as well (good and bad). As they gained control over law enforcement, gradually, the same "slave master" mentality that many whites held in the early South in the U.S. when slavery thrived, has transcended to north of the Mason-Dixon line (the Ohio river), and into the minds of these newly minted policeman, sheriffs, and deputies in the northern cities of the U.S. (and not into just those Irish minds, but German minds, Italian minds, and other European immigrant communities). Ironically, they *were* immigrants, but in this current day and time many are not very nice to those whom we currently refer to as "immigrants". They forget that they were treated the same way when they first arrived in America.

But me and my family are Black, Catholic, AND of Irish heritage! This mixed heritage was always a challenge for me growing up, and was probably even more troubling for many of my family ancestors during this time, and ideally for my father and the Kinneys particularly. They say that when you mix black and white blood, the black gene is the dominant gene and therefore, you're considered black… every time in America. However, all of my Kinney aunts and uncles have green eyes, are extremely light-skinned, and most have light brown or red hair. So, their appearance was probably startling and maybe even troublesome for many in the Black community at the time. They all definitely look like they have Irish blood in them (I have the same features too and know about these prejudices across races where you receive it on both sides: not white enough, and never black enough). I'm sure all the Kinneys received a lot of this flack back in the troubled U.S. racial times of the 50s and 60s.

Later in life, I began to learn more about the racial struggles of Black families that we knew in Cincinnati (mine included) and families like ours all over America who were not allowed basic rights, couldn't live or work where they wanted, and had to contend with many personal challenges in dealing with white supremacy, all because of the color of their skin. Thinking back, it's now connecting that my father, among many other Black men of his time in particular that were highly impacted by racial issues of his time. Black men were told often by whites that they are "not a man" and not important, and really all Blacks were treated as "sub-human" then. And then decades later, the same sentiments appeared to still be there; I would return to Cincinnati to experience the same thing myself first-hand as an adult, history repeating itself.

Prejudice is truly ugly whenever it rears its ugly head, whether as a child or as an adult. And as a Black person, whether you're reading/hearing about someone experiencing the harshness and evil of prejudice, or you're observing and witnessing it in front of you, or if you're experiencing it first-hand yourself, it causes an immense amount of mental strain and pressure on the human psyche. Blacks for decades and decades in America have been diminished as human beings, they are expected not to have a sense of well-being. The impression is that Blacks are *supposed* to suffer and take it without feeling anything, without reacting, with no repercussions or accountability at the hands of the perpetrator. When really the result has repeatedly been inevitable chronic stress, anxiety, depression, substance abuse, destructive behavior, and even suicide. Yes, some think (and might be right) that death has got to be better than being under this level of scrutiny or this level of oppression. And that was the case of many of those slaves trying to cross the Ohio river in the dead of winter.

But African-Americans are a people full of hope... we have been for generations; it is part of our faith to know that God is always with us. *Any* people who can survive the Middle Passage (the trip from Africa through atrocious conditions on slave ships), who can survive 400 years of slavery and oppression (picking cotton and physically building up this country while receiving no credit for doing so), and who still are systematically being held back from various basic opportunities deserving of any human being (e.g., food, housing, education, security, etc.) – this population of people should be commended and rewarded for enduring such strife. And yet we are still thriving as a people! We press on *and* we prosper in spite of all these hurdles – just amazing!

> *"And we know that all things work together for good to them that love God, to them who are called according to His purpose…. What shall we then say to these things? If God be for us, who can be against us?"* – **Romans 8:28-31**

Yet there are many stories of African-Americans in our community who have suffered more than others - some of the effects long-lasting and harsh. I believe that my family falls into this category unfortunately, and on this topic, I want to provide some introspection. We have seen how these things have negatively affected families and communities in ways unimaginable – that is when I began to think about in my own family, and how I now want to search my family's story in this regard. **What prejudice did we experience because of how we looked? Did the prejudice that we experienced in my own hometown progress similarly in other cities across America?** According to what happened on January 6, 2021, the answer to that question is probably a resounding "Yes!"

It is just so sad and unfortunate that such racial strife continues across our country to this day, and it goes well beyond Cincinnati, Ohio. It is truly a major flaw of our country that requires constant prayer. Only something as big as God can surmount all that evil in all those hearts that stormed the Capitol Building on January 6, 2021 (and all those whom they know with the same sentiment who were not in attendance in DC that day). Only God can save us all. Like many of my African-American ancestors, I am ever-hopeful and prayerful for the best intentions and actions of every American on-going.

Chapter 3:

Life in Evanston – An Idyllic Life

*"For I will have respect unto you, and make you fruitful, and multiply you, and establish my covenant with you." – **Leviticus 26:9***

B efore we grew up on Grantwood we lived on Irving Street in the Colonial Apartments right off Forest Avenue in the Avondale section of Cincinnati. My brothers have fond memories of living "by the dumpster" and frequently eating toast and tea to get by. They told me that (and I learned over time) that the early 60s was a very turbulent time across the U.S. in many Black communities, ours included. It was a time of protests, sit-ins, and "freedom riders" (protesters who went to different parts of the South to protest and challenge racial laws in the U.S. at the time, some of them young white college students from the Cincinnati area). So, they were cautioned by my parents where they could and could not go across Cincinnati. By the time we moved into 1607 Grantwood Avenue in Evanston in 1962, my mother had just found out she was pregnant with me, her *ninth* child. Therefore, a dwelling the size of a house was definitely in order, and from what I hear all of my sibling were ecstatic about moving into a house from the crowded apartment they had before.

Life in the Evanston community in Cincinnati was truly idyllic, because we had all that we needed. We were not rich, but we grew up in a time when the community raised our children together and we all looked after one another. If you got in trouble down the street, you got scolded there, then the neighbor would call your parents, and you got scolded a second time when you arrived home!

Our house was a quaint two-story home on Grantwood Avenue in Evanston. You had to take two flights of steps (one cement, then one wooden) to get to the large front porch that was (eventually) screened in. To the right of the front porch was a cement patio over the garage where my brother Carl (a year older than me) and I would climb up and down repeatedly (just because we could. I remember it was part of our obstacle course going around the house. We had a small front yard that was cut in half by the steps that led to the front porch. After climbing the first flight of steps going up to the house, there was a cement path to the left that took you all the way around the side to the back of the house, passing by the back-cellar door (something we had to keep secured from neighborhood crooks), and the cement path extended all the way to the set of steps out back that led to the house's back door.

When you stepped into 1607 Grantwood the first room you encountered was the living room; then to the right was the dining room and lots of hardwood flooring. Both rooms were big (or at least they seemed that way when I was growing up), and they were the focal point of our family gatherings. In the living room was a "Hi-Fi Stereo" that looked like a wooden box with a built-in speaker on the side. When you lifted the lid, inside was the turntable and all of Daddy's LP records with artists like Billy Eckstine, Johnny Mathis, and my mom's favorite: Dionne Warwick. When Daddy and Mom played the records, we'd all end up dancing in the middle of the living room floor... a lot of family fun. Carl and I ended up dancing with Daddy as we balanced on top of his feet, and Mom would teach the rest of us the "Cha-Cha". (Little did I know that this was my first lesson in Latino culture right in my own living room taught by my mom, and I am now fluent in Spanish!) I have a lot of fond memories of my Mom, Daddy, me and all my siblings spending many fun days and nights there in the living room dancing to that Hi-Fi Stereo. I remember Daddy would play Johnny Mathis' "A Hundred Thousand Bubbles" song over and over while singing it, to me and my brother Carl's delight. He treated us like twins, often scooping us both up off the ground simultaneously and holding us up high on his tall frame. I remember caressing his soft, curly hair as he did so. He was always singing, humming, or whistling. These are the few fond memories that I have of Daddy as we grew up on Grantwood.

I also remember Daddy being meticulous about cleanliness, something he got from his mother (Grandmother Kinney). I know, because her house was always spotless when we visited. Daddy would give each of us chores to keep the house clean, and he would wash his own hands and face several times a day. He was quite the family man, loading us all in our big pink station wagon to go to the park, the drive-in, to get ice cream, or to visit family on Sundays. And Mom always followed his lead regarding the rules of the house and the way it all was run.

As we grew up on Grantwood, the girls stayed upstairs on the second floor, my parents had a bedroom on the first floor, and the boys stayed in the remodeled basement. Our basement was our "rec room" with a tiled linoleum floor where we roller skated, where my brothers set up elaborate train sets or Hot Wheels tracks, and where we did a lot of dancing and game playing. We would play the radio downstairs and dance our line dances, or play "Hot Beans for Supper". "Hot Beans for Supper", by the way, was a game where one of us asked everyone to close their eyes. That person would then hide a coiled belt, and then send us to find it. When/if anyone found the belt, THAT person would proceed to whoop us all with the belt until the last person scaled the top bed of one of the two sets of bunk beds we had in the basement for my four brothers. It sounds cruel, but it was a LOT of fun! We also did dangerous stuff like making each other "go to sleep" by cutting off our oxygen and watching the person squirm until they gained full consciousness. We later found out that this is something that could have killed any one of us, but these were the kinds of "secret" activities" that we siblings would do in group fashion in our "rec room". This is why all of my cousins on the Kinney and Robinson side of my family LOVED to come to our house: a lot of kids, a lot of music and dancing, good eating, and a LOT of fun and interesting activities, like our house-wide hide and seek games. My cousins *really* loved coming over during the holidays especially, because we'd be doing even *more* activities in our basement. It's where my entire family went to have a good time. Even my Mom would go down there with my aunts to listen to Redd Foxx's comedy albums (as if the kids could not hear it upstairs!). We went down there to skate, play, do the laundry, to clean catfish after my brothers went fishing, and to wash the dog. It's also the place where you could be taken by Daddy (or Mom) if you were getting a whooping!

Upstairs on the second floor of the house where the girls slept, it was always pristine, neat, and clean. The boys would rarely come upstairs unless they absolutely had to or needed something from one of us. My sisters and I always kept upstairs neater and cleaner than the way my brothers maintained the basement. We wanted no one to invade our "territory". We ALL, on the other hand, often went to the basement for recreation, and the laundry room was down there too. So, we all eventually were forced to go to the basement often, whether we wanted to or not. But my brothers were used to the company down there. Also, our laundry chute went from the first-floor bathroom to the basement. It's hard to believe that my brother Carl and I were slender enough to climb through this chute and did so regularly to play, run, and hide from one another.

The first floor was where my Mom and dad's bedroom was, and it was discipline central. You heard some kind of advice whenever you walked in that front door. We all had to pass through that "gauntlet of wisdom" (enter the front door and pass Mom and Daddy's room) before proceeding upstairs or downstairs (although you could sneak around through the dining room to get upstairs, but you would definitely be heard through the 5 small rooms on that first floor). To this day, I wonder how we all fit into that house. I have gone back to visit the house since, which is still standing and in good condition, thank goodness. But when I see it now, it's amazing to try to visually retrofit all of us in there. Somehow our parents made it work.

We were all pretty crowded in that house on Grantwood, but I loved it being the youngest! There was never a dull moment, always someone around to talk to, another family member or guest to join us for dinner (although the table was already full of people!). My Mom and dad often welcomed cousins and other family members to live with us when they fell on hard times. I would always ask "Where are they gonna sleep?!" I slept with each of my sisters, and did not have my own bed until I was about 10 years old (even then, only after some siblings moved out). To this day, I have no idea how my dad, Robert Lee "Buddy" Kinney, Sr. and my Mom, Alfreda Robinson Kinney raised nine children on Grantwood in Evanston. That alone was a miracle.

One Friday afternoon, Daddy came bounding up the front steps and into the house with such excitement, his big feet sounded like an elephant was entering our little home. Mom later told me that Daddy used his big frame and large feet to test the strength of our house as they considered it for purchase. He went from floor to floor (and on each stairwell landing) and jumped up and down to see how strong the structure was. When it passed his "jumping" test, they agreed to buy the house on Grantwood. On this day, I heard Daddy's "jumping" feet take two steps at a time to scale our front steps to the house.

"Freda! Freda!" he exclaimed, "I got the job at Heekin!" Daddy was so happy to move beyond the low-paying elevator operator job he had held at the Shillito's Building in the very conservative downtown Cincinnati, Ohio. Heekin Canning Company was a large canning manufacturer and process plant that was situated on the west side of downtown Cincinnati. Many black men, those who had not been drafted, worked in this canning factory. They canned tuna, beans, soup, tobacco, beer... anything that was sold in a can in that area of the country. The West End, near where Heekin was located, is where the Robinsons (my mother's brother, Gus, and his wife Mary) lived with their eleven kids. That's how the families did it back then: these big Catholic families had a LOT of kids! We were no different. The Robinsons lived in the West End community, downtown Cincinnati, which was considered a rough neighborhood then. My Mom was also from a family of nine kids (plus two kids who went to foster care), so there were a lot of Robinsons. My dad had fourteen siblings!... so needless to say, there are a LOT of Kinney's too. We all had the run of Cincinnati, Ohio at the time, in the late sixties. But it was our trips to the West End to visit the Robinsons that proved to be a lot of fun, a learning experience for us coming from the more modest Evanston community, and a good employment opportunity for Daddy.

My parents had been struggling quite a bit to feed all nine of us, and to maintain the home they had just purchased two years after I was born. Daddy got the job at Heekin, because my Uncle Gus had put in a good word there, the place where he had been working for five years, taking care of his large family in the West End. He immediately called his brother-in-law to give him the good news: "Gus, I got the job! I'll be working with you now!"

So, Daddy went to work with Uncle Gus, in the fall of 1965. Charles "Gus", my Uncle Bill – Adolf Robinson, my mother, her twin brother Alfred, and all nine of the Robinsons grew up on the "West End" side of Cincinnati, a very industrial part of the city loaded with factories where many of them worked.

Once Daddy started working vigorously at Heekin, it would tire him. My Uncle Bill ("Unk", as we affectionately called him), later told me "Mom was Daddy's past time". When he got home from work from the canning company each day, if he ("Unk") was sitting at the kitchen table talking with "Sissy" (my Mom), "Buddy" would arrive home from work and call her name. Whether they were in mid-conversation or not, Mom would excuse herself and go into the bedroom with her husband... End of conversation. "Unk" told me that they were madly in love with each other, so Mom would always oblige "Buddy's" every request. The needs of her husband and children were always her priority, and for some (like her siblings) that was a challenge.

Everyone in the neighborhood knew of our large Catholic family. I heard that my Mom would get teased while walking down the street with her many children holding onto her skirt to stay in line. "There goes Freda with all them damn kids!" they'd say. There were other black families in the neighborhood with whom we were very close that also had many children: The Berries, Robinsons, Jacksons, Warners, and Browns. Mr. and Mrs. Thurston Howell were my godparents ("Pops" was such a flirt with all the young women in the neighborhood!), and they lived two doors down from the Berries who were right across the street from us. *(Mrs. Berry died in 2021 also; may this loving woman rest in heavenly peace after living to 93 and seeing many generations after her.)* Mrs. Bradshaw was the "mean lady" who lived in the middle of the block and told on us all the time, but her kids were nice (Tara and Marcelle).

We had other black families we mingled with in the neighborhood, like the Banks family on Montgomery Road near St. Mark (Valerie was my fun play buddy, and I would pass through the parking lot of the Liberal's Grocery store and through Mrs. Johnson's back yard to get to her house. Her brother Jeff was a good friend of my brothers Fran and Chico. "Val" and I would ride our bikes in the Liberal parking lot without fear. Mrs. Johnson at the time had a cognitively challenged daughter named Connie. I loved to play with Connie when my Mom would visit Mrs. Johnson, and they would sit and talk over coffee. One day I visited Connie on my own on the way to the Bank's house. This particular day Connie was energized, I'm sure seeing me added to her excitement. When inside, we began to play. She got more and more excited and "happy"… so happy that she proceeded to pick up their 20" TV and toss it like a ball across the room. It slammed to the floor and tore into pieces to Mrs. Johnson's horror and to our shock! Connie and I both froze and looked at Mrs. Johnson for her reaction, which was to snatch Connie's arm and make her sit in an armchair nearby. Then she ushered me to the door, letting me know that our playtime had indeed ended. I still have fond memories of playing with Connie more after that, but not sure how she faired in adulthood as I went off to high school and college. But she and a few other girls in the neighborhood were part of these other black families we all grew up with in this small community of Evanston, just about 5 miles north of downtown Cincinnati. At one time it was an affluent white Catholic community until blacks began moving into Evanston in the late 60s. The Banks, the Johnsons, the Lattimores, and our family were some of the many black families who moved in and made this a nice close-knit community for a number of black Catholic families, who also attended St. Mark Catholic Church and School.

The Robinsons lived up the street; Deneen Robinson was/is my best, best friend in the world. We had long talks about life, challenges with our parents, school, and about our growth into womanhood. We would have seances with our ancestors, and she taught me how to tie my shoes and how to strike a match (the match-striking was a very scary thing for me when I was growing up). The Berrys across the street included Monica Berry, although a little older than me, she became a very good friend to me. She taught me a lot about boys (since I went to a private all-girls high school, I didn't mingle a lot with the boys in the neighborhood, but she educated me on that and the streets of Cincinnati). Deneen and I would join up to go to the local Royale Skating Rink *every* weekend in our teen years to skate our hearts out. These were the families of my friends, and my siblings had friends that belonged to those other families on the block also (e.g., the Johnsons, the Lattimores, the Warners, the other Banks family - their Mom Laura was our school secretary, the Chunns, etc.). So needless to say, we were all close-knit families not only on Grantwood, but all across the community of Evanston in Cincinnati, Ohio.

Grantwood was indeed an idyllic place for a young, black child of the Midwest at the time. We huddled together during the tough winters and blizzards that occurred then. In the summer we would wait for the ice cream man (truck) to come around; you know, the one that served the *real* soft-serve ice cream on a cone where he could even mix chocolate and vanilla on the cone! And we would scream when we heard the twinkling musical sound coming from the ice cream truck as it would near our neighborhood:

"I scream, you scream, we all scream for ice cream!" We could not wait until Fourth of July to play in the street with our sparklers in our new 4ᵗʰ of July outfits (often sewed by mom). We normally had to be in the house when the street light came on, but some nights in the summer, we were allowed to hang late, run in our neighbors' sprinklers, and/or play games in the street under the light with the other kids. And then the nights when all the kids were in the street under the street light, we would play games (like Red Light, Green Light and Red Rover). Since Grantwood was a side street off Woodburn Avenue in Evanston, we did not have to worry about too much traffic breaking up our games. It was a peaceful and safe time in our neighborhood when we could sleep out on our front porch, and ride our bikes freely around the community of Evanston, sometimes barefoot. Sometimes the peace was broken up occasionally by a fight between friends and/or even between some family members who lived on Grantwood. Some of those family fights even spilled out onto the street for us all to see (and what a sight it was!), so we really were ALL family in that regard. Other than that, it was a generally peaceful and relatively innocent existence growing up there, but did resemble a kind of "Peyton Place" with some kind of drama in the atmosphere of the community throughout every season.

It was also a troublesome time for the country just off the heels of the Vietnam war in the late 60's, for our small, close-knit community of Evanston with all the prejudice in Cincinnati (and across the country) against the Black community. It definitely became a problem for my young parents with so many children. I was too young to realize it at the time, but there were many marches for Civil Rights and many clashes with those deep-rooted racists of the time. Although we lived right next to a very prejudiced part of town called Norwood, we never experienced too much of this on Grantwood in Evanston, or so it seemed to many of us young black Catholic children as we ran off to attend St. Mark School and Church just blocks away from Norwood. Now that I look back, I realize that we were a bit sheltered. The Evanston community, which had more residential housing, was a bit more "uptown" than the West End (which contained many housing projects in Cincinnati full of smaller apartment units). Evanston had a pretty good reputation for being safe, clean, and relatively free of crime. But like any other black community of Cincinnati, Ohio at that time, Evanston was under a lot more stress from both poverty and racism than we ever realized at that time. The prejudice and oppression of basic needs would affect us greatly and especially my father.

My parents' relationship deteriorated over time, as life got hard for Daddy in many different ways living in Cincinnati, resulting from all the oppression that spread across the entire Black community. All this "interference" affected their passion for one another, not to mention the challenges of raising a large Black family during this time in America. Their encounters went from warm hugs and loving conversations to "spirited discussions" that turned into large shouting matches in front of us, the children.

They eventually had more and more arguments prompted by Daddy's frustrations in life, and Mom trying to manage him and her many children simultaneously. All this transitioned into a time of hard living for "Buddy" and "Sissy"… not so much love and passion and no serenading any more. I always wondered (and would later ask Mom) "Why did you all stop having kids with me? Why didn't you have *ten* kids?" I later realized a lot was going on between my parents and also within the Black community at that time. The combination of environmental factors made it hard (always has) for Black families to stay together. At this time (and still is today to some) the sentiment was that Black families were not supposed to thrive; they were *supposed* to struggle, which is perpetuating slave mentality among us all, still stuck in our ugly past and not able to move forward positively.

But besides all these outside factors, my father had a secret he was holding inside… something was troubling him quite a bit (and none of us, except my Mom knew of it and understood it). He happily accepted that job working with Uncle Gus at the Heekin Canning Company years earlier, but what he thought was the start of a wonderful place in time for him and his family would eventually become hell on earth for us all.

On some occasions, we would see Daddy and Mom in the kitchen (early 60s) with a house full of children running around, and Daddy in a stupor over his cup of coffee. "Buddy? Buddy? What's wrong?" Mom would ask (no answer). It was then that Mom knew that the times and conditions in Evanston (and the black community in general) in Cincinnati were changing, and it would greatly affect her, her husband, and her children. It must have been an awfully difficult time for Mom... I feel for her. She probably knew then that she would be in for a long, hard ride with her husband's mental state, and that she would have to be strong for him and for her children. She had no idea how strong she (and all of us) would have to be...

Chapter 4:

The Kids of King

"God will never place on you more than you can handle"... this is a phrase that has been repeated to me in a lot of trying times in my life (especially during my teen years). And many trying times we have had indeed. St. Teresa of Avila (a famous Spanish Carmelite nun well-known in the Catholic faith) once stated "To have courage for whatever comes in life – everything lies in that." And one thing I have learned painfully over the years is that, regardless of your circumstances in life, you *can* overcome those challenges if your mind is focused on love, commitment to yourself, an insistence on being happy in life, and most importantly, faith in God. Great points of vulnerability in our lives can bring about change and hopefully inspiration for others, but it was definitely my siblings and my faith that have kept me strong throughout my whole life. Without each, I don't know how I could have survived everything that was about to come at me over the next few years of my young life. But nothing in life is too hard if it brings us into God's Will for you in your life (I would later find out).

Growing up in the poor but respectable community of Evanston, I experienced a great range of emotions, from being a happy and ignorantly blissful child to one that was traumatized by tragedy twice over. But when I really think about it and weigh all the good and the bad, growing up I/we actually did just fine, considering it all. We were all well-disciplined, well mannered, well-nourished, and Catholic school educated. My parent's offspring consisted of nine children within eleven years' time. From oldest to youngest are ("Bobby" or Robert Lee, Jr., Karen Marie, "Chico" or Alfred, Francis Wayne, Angela Jewel, Cecilia Ann, Cynthia Elaine, Carl Vincent, and "the baby" me – Naomi Joan). We got teased about not having a television for entertainment, so, you know what came next for my dad! Those were the more simplistic times of my upbringing before I (later) realized what had transpired in 1967 it threw our innocent, idyllic family lifestyle off course...

First before I tell you about my loving parents and their challenges, let me introduce to you my eight precious siblings. Each of them had/have vastly different personalities although we were born not more than two years apart at the most. And yes, I get a little ahead of myself a bit in telling you about each of my siblings before I tell you details of my parents. Some of what I'll tell you transpired *after* the deaths of my parents. But it gives you some insight into their personalities and how we have developed our strong sibling bond over the years. They are my BFFs – Best Friends Forever in this life, considering what we've been through together; I look to them for everything in life – always have, always will.

Before I tell you about each sibling, here is a list of our birth order and birth dates so you can see how close we are in birth order (and to show the amazing feat my mother did of giving birth to us all). Some of my older siblings told me later in life that "Mom was always coming home with a baby in her arms and/or was always pregnant", so we are many and we know that love was abundant among our parents. Bear with me, as I define *my* perception of my sweet siblings as we grew up in Cincinnati and (a bit beyond) from the "baby sis" point of view (quite a group of characters, myself included). We have surmounted SO much together; we could not have done it without helping one another... a fact we all realize is evident to this day.

Name *(from the oldest to youngest)*	**Birthdate**
Robert "Bobby" Lee Kinney, Jr.	January 22, 1953
Karen "Kay" Marie Kinney	January 9, 1954
Alfred "Chico" Kinney	January 21, 1956
Francis "Fran" Wayne Kinney	January 29, 1957
Angela "Ang" Jewel Kinney	February 23, 1958
Cecilia "Ceal" Ann Kinney	July 16, 1959

Cynthia "Cindy" Elaine Kinney	April 15, 1961
Carl Vincent Kinney	May 7, 1962
Naomi "Nay" Joan Kinney	August 17, 1963

My Precious Siblings

"Bobby" (Robert Jr.) was truly "a Big Brother" who watched over all his numerous younger siblings with great pride and confidence. He was a man whose thunderous voice, his great intelligence and wisdom, and his love for chess made him stand out from many of the younger "brothers" in the hood at the time. I don't remember him getting into so much trouble with my parents as my other brothers. He seemed to know he was the leader and always had to be a good role model to us all. But I'm sure he had his share of run-ins with my older siblings in his earlier years before I was born. He was tall, dark and handsome, athletic (loved softball and bowled like crazy, did both in leagues in Cincinnati), and gorgeous and he wore a huge afro like the Jackson Five wore back in the 60s and 70s. He was very smart too, always excelling in school and getting good grades. Everyone (including us) knew he was the leader of the siblings in our family, and he reveled in this being the proud, confident person he was. I remember in his 20s he wore this black leather jacket with white fur around the collar, tight bell-bottom blue jeans, and platform shoes (with the big afro, looking like "Shaft").

He, like my father, was a lover of music, and always had his radio blasting in our remodeled basement, which was considered the boys' room in our house. Once when I was a busy, youngster always in search of what my siblings were up to, I noticed that the lights were out in the basement, but the Isley Brother's "Work to Do" was blasting from the radio in the basement. I was curious, so I ran downstairs and quickly cut on the lights. Standing there naked and dancing was my brother Bobby, and it was a bit shocking for us both. He dropped to the floor pallets, and began grabbing clothes toward the front of him to hide his private parts from his little sister. Why he was there dancing naked I have no idea, but when I think back on it, it was probably very liberating for him (especially without his other brothers crowding his space). I cut the lights back off, and ran upstairs telling myself "next time I'll give a shout out before I go down there and cut on the lights so fast!"

For many years my eldest sibling worked at (and retired from) the Ford Motor Company in the Evendale section of Cincinnati doing assembly line work, and then went to his bowling league meet up at Madison Bowl in Cincinnati (a place where we all grew up doing a LOT of bowling). After work he would occasionally stop by Grantwood on the way home to his own apartment to see what his Mom and younger siblings were up to. On one funny occasion, "Bobcat" (as he was affectionately called by his buddies) drove up to Mom's house on Grantwood when he was older and owned a big black shiny Pontiac Catalina that he always kept spotless. When he arrived in front of the house where I was often playing, he smelled my sister Cindy's chocolate chip cookies cooking in the kitchen. He mounted the steps in front of Grantwood two at a time scaling the two sets of steps that led up to our house, and he made it to the kitchen where cookies were cooling on the counter. Cindy (the family domesticate was always in the kitchen preparing something just like Mom) was there preparing cookies. She looked at him (anticipating his next move), he looked at her and then at the cookies. Then he proceeded to grab about a half dozen cookies in each hand and took off running toward the front door. He blasted through the front door, and what happened next turned out to be one of the funniest stories that all of my siblings, and we still laugh about to this day: Bobby ran out of the house and made it down the first flight of steps, with Cindy in close chase behind him. My cousin, Darrell, and I were sitting at the bottom of the steps after playing a mean game of step ball, as we often did to pass the time, and had full view of the course of events about to unfold. Seeing Bobby dashing out the door, we quickly stepped aside to let Bob complete the last set of six steps to finish his escape. His platform shoes failed to support him, though, and he proceeded to slide and bump on his rump, slide and bump on his rump, slide and bump on the rump all the way down the rest of the steps... scraping up his back, tearing up his elbows!! The cookies eventually crumbled right in his hands from his grip and they ended up all over the cement stairs where we were playing step ball, where then sat my brother Bob looking totally busted and disgusted... and injured!! Regardless of his howls of pain (from his elbows), Cindy started whacking at him, and boy, did he deserve it! He ruined the cookies we ALL had been waiting for! He was normally a very serious person (at least around me, he was), but he got his clown on a few times, like on this occasion which was both memorable and funny.

For high school, Bob attended a prestigious all-boys school in Cincinnati (Xavier High School) and then graduated with honors from Xavier University (a Jesuit university), which was just blocks away from our home in Evanston. He even studied to be a priest at one point. Later, what I found as I grew up is that he was a true leader and showed those skills greatly, particularly after my parents died. Having a big heart, he adopted two children in his life (Tikoa Kinney and Ashley Kinney). Robert Kinney, III (Little Bobby) my second-born nephew was his only offspring. He was a great counselor, a father-figure to me often, and the rock of our family. He placed the laurel leaf crown on my head at my graduation from Ursuline Academy of Cincinnati in 1981 standing in that day as my father (a moment I'll never forget). He often stood in as my father and even into my adulthood he was the true counselor, always taking my late-night phone calls and advising me accordingly. He died an accidental death in January, 2001, shocking us, breaking our hearts, and creating a great hole in our family structure, definitely among me and my siblings. When I returned to DC from his funeral in Cincinnati, I found out that I was expecting my daughter Julia; God giveth and He taketh. Years later in 2019 his son Robert III died after a long battle with kidney disease. Now all three "Roberts" are gone: My father Robert Lee Kinney, Sr.; my brother Robert Lee Kinney, Jr.; and my nephew Robert Lee Kinney, III. May their souls rest in heavenly peace. Bobby was called "the Professor" by my mother's brother, Uncle Adolf "Bill" Robinson.

Karen my eldest sister, like Bobby, often played surrogate parent (sometimes a stand in as my mother or being the 2nd Mom to help or assist our Mom) for/with her younger siblings. Always wearing her cheerful Pepsodent smile and always thinking positively in every situation life can bring, I've seen her go through many challenges in life and come out shining on the other side. She's a true testament of endurance and perseverance in life. When I was young in particular, I always perceived my sister Karen as a young black politically active woman, a musical artist (she used to play the guitar), a creative-artist (she has led me and my siblings through many craft, art, and painting projects, and proud of her black heritage and family. Like Bobby, she used to wear a big, beautiful afro (all the kids did then to symbolize the Black power struggle), and she was always smiling and walking with her head up in great confidence, showing off her beautiful, flawless caramel-colored skin while she would wear her matching Coca-Cola bell-bottom jeans and a vest often on her then very shapely young figure (she wore a lot of cut-off blue jean shorts too). She was my beautiful, cool, groovy, and hippie-like big sister, who I liked to hear playing her guitar, singing praise songs from our church, and hanging artistic things in her room over her bed upstairs in our house on Grantwood.

I will never forget when "Kay" used to take me with her to Big Sister Day at St. Ursula and to their Christmas Program each year; I would look forward to it! At her all-girls Catholic high school, she was one of the first few blacks in our neighborhood to attend that school which ironically was located right in the neighboring Walnut Hills neighborhood (another predominantly African-American community in Cincinnati). That must have been VERY challenging during that time to be "one of the firsts", but she and a few other girls from St. Mark were highly recommended by Sr. Rose Helene Wildehaus (principal at St. Mark and an angel to our family often as I grew up). So, our Catholic connections helped make that happen. She was always such a good, positive, inspirational, and helpful big sister especially on those days we spent together at her high school: so full of sisterly love and the holiday spirit, showing me off to all of her classmates, and spending one-on-one time with me doing crafty projects there. She could create, build, decorate, and paint *anything* creatively. She often sang and played her guitar during mass at St. Mark. And I remember her always keeping a stash of sweet candies hidden (like green Jolly Ranchers) to share with me on special occasions when she knew her "baby sister" really needed it. She was a big sister that I loved looking up too, so feminine and so in control of her body, mind, her skills, and her spirit. She made growing up in some of our more difficult circumstances light-hearted and surmountable.

Karen taught me a lot of my first skills and almost had to force them onto me, knowing my capabilities better than

I knew them myself – she always believed in me and had confidence in me. The first time I went roller skating, Karen took me, and I remember her pushing me out onto the floor (since I would not let go of the wall initially). After a few falls, you could not get me out of the roller-skating rink! I became obsessed with skating in the following years, and it turned out to be a good, clean activity for me at the time as a teenager. Karen was also my guide (and Carl's) at summer camps during the summer. She got a summer job at Camp Cartwright in Kentucky, and Carl and I were campers there. That is where I first dove into the deep end of the pool, all by her coaxing and guiding me. After demonstrating the basic feet first jump into the deep water, it took Karen a while to get me to even walk out onto the diving board. Then she got in the water, and I stood there looking down as she treaded water below and shouted "Just jump, Nay! You'll come right back up! Jump! Jump!" I knew how to swim a little, but this would be a big step for me. But my big sister was there to catch me, so trustingly, I jumped. And sure enough, she was right there when I plunged back to the surface as she had promised would occur. I felt such a great sense of accomplishment that day and had much greater confidence. This is just one example of how my siblings have forced me to learn things for my own good, and I have trusted their guidance. In this they all have rarely failed me.

"Kay" was also one of our family members (per my experience) that kept us culturally diverse and helped us to think beyond Cincinnati, Ohio and beyond the U.S. She studied

French in high school, and did very well learning that foreign language. She also was the sister wearing dashikis (African style print shirts that were popular among young African-Americans at the time, especially those who were into civil rights activism). One year she offered to have a travel abroad student from Africa named "Effie" who came to live with us during his studies. It was a very interesting experience to see someone from another country living in our house. I remember I would marvel at his ability to switch from speaking English to French and back. He told us a lot of what we had they did not have in his village in Africa, and he was fascinated at how we pressed all of our clothes (especially our Catholic school uniforms). Effie learned a lot about living in America, but we learned a lot from his as well.

Karen moved away from us to study at the University of Detroit, the first one of us to bravely "fly the coop" to go to college. She lived in Detroit for a while, and she married a really cool white guy named Michael Malek. They lived on the second level of a roomy two-family flat, and eventually two kids came on the scene (Jonathan, the first nephew in our family, and then Jennifer came shortly after). My Mom would allow us (and older siblings) to take occasional Greyhound bus trips there to see them, especially during Thanksgiving breaks, and "Kay" would do fun crafty projects. Once we made colorful, clear plastic flowers from acrylic liquid, and another time we drew on plastic panels, and cut out the pictures she baked them in the oven, and then they became jewelry/earrings). She would also bake bread and we would help, and it was a true delight to see our culinary results. They later divorced, and Karen moved back to Cincinnati with her two children Jonathan and Jennifer, and shortly after, life for her became somewhat challenging as a single Mom in the often snow-ridden Detroit. I remember I was by the phone when Mom told her "Come on home; bring those children home, baby." I was glad she did tell her to do that. She was the first of my sisters I directly observed having and raising a baby, and seeing her as a mother amazed me and showed me a lot about how to manage babies/children while I was a young impressionable pre-teen. Karen, and a very young Jonathan and Jennifer arrived at our home on Grantwood that summer in the mid-70s when disco was hot (along with the weather I remember). I felt like our family was growing again. Karen and her kids stayed with us on Grantwood for several months until "Kay" eventually got her own place and they moved out. She went on to hold a host of community service focused jobs around the Cincinnati area like at Community Chest, helping others, which is the same thing she is so good at to this day. She is ideal to working in the social services industry for her compassionate spirit, generous actions, and warm personality when greeting anyone.

Now that Jonathan and Jennifer are grown and have their own families, I see that Kay has blossomed into a wonderful grandmother, so ever maternal as always, something I know she got from our Mom(especially her ability to cook so well). She's a really good grandmother to her grandchildren, and she always revels in being with *all* of our family. Despite having gone through such adversity, she still has the same jovial, positive, calm, self-assured, loving spirit as if she let problems roll off her shoulders like raindrops on a slicker. And she has always been committed to her faith and to her family (just like our Mom in many ways... she must have been watching and observing Mom persevere as well). She has proven that commitment to family time and to us frequently over the years. Now, the eldest living sibling, she is now our new family matriarch who leads us ever-positively, spiritually, and with conviction.

"Alfred" (we call him "Al" or "Chico") was always the rambunctious little boy growing up on Grantwood, who ran a vigorous paper route as a boy (and loved it!). He has always been a "hustler" in one way or another, strong as an ox, full of positivity, and quite the protector of our family also... another "Big Brother." Chico and Fran (the next sibling in line) have always been close and were common in their activities at home and beyond. These two have always been the best story tellers in our clan. They've been the family clowns, the standouts, always full of energy and in the middle of the Kinney spotlight. But Al has always been more clever and cunning in many ways, sometimes being a detriment to himself in the process.... Thinking maybe that he's a little TOO clever.... Never more-clever than our Mom though! "Chico" has always had an incredible amount of personal confidence in himself and the physical endurance to back it up. After playing and competing with his brothers in our front yard, he eventually played football in high school at Purcell Catholic High School (then for boys only), and he also liked to lift weights that he kept in the basement of our house (and looked the part). All of my female friends used to comment in admiration, "Wow, is HE your brother?" At about 5'10" with a stocky build, cocoa brown skin, handsome chiseled face (like my father), super slender waist *then* to go with it all, he always dressed meticulously, and looked good in whatever he wore (which is also what I heard about our father: that his stature made the clothes look good).

However, as a young rebellious teen, he (and Fran, sometimes together) constantly challenged my Mom and her ability to oversee our home as a single mother, coming home whenever he wanted to and bringing in whatever/whomever he wanted, much to the chagrin of my Mom. Typical of the times when many young black men did not have many opportunities to be as productive as they could, my older brothers instead often got into meddlesome stuff in our neighborhood (much influenced by their friends in the neighborhood). Some things they got into were for rather minor, like pulling the local street fire alarms (when those were on every other street corner along with real telephone booths and the large cans of rock salt for use in winter months - but the local kids not attended to would commonly meddle with all these things until these regular street-corner staples became extinct in Cincinnati). Chico and Fran would often run together with the same group of young men in our neighborhood (e.g., "Lou", "Crack", "Nate", etc.), and could often be found playing basketball in our driveway where we had a hoop, playing cards in our basement, or hanging out at places in the hood like nearby Jonathan Park.

One day Chico and Fran came home with a hoard of big brown boxes that they said "fell off" the train. Next to the Coca-Cola plant near our home were some railroad tracks that helped that company with the distribution of soda ("pop" as we call it in Ohio and throughout the Mid-West) across the region. Chico and Fran had happened upon the boxes that had fallen from a passing train that was loaded with King Vitamin cereal (remember, King Vitamin "Have breakfast with the King!" commercials?). Well, my two brothers showed up at our house each with a HUGE box that contained several boxes of King Vitamin cereal! And this was good, considering the fact that Chico and Fran ate cereal from mixing bowls regularly (something that my mother hated, yelling "I have NINE children to feed!"). But now they had enough cereal to last for a while! They came through the door with all that cereal like they had really hit the lottery! (We surely thought so as kids who love cereal!) These are the kinds of antics that my brothers used to get into growing up in our neighborhood like pulling those local fire alarms and running... Seemingly minor compared to what the young men get into these days. It drove my mother crazy having to deal with this while raising so many other children too.

Once when Chico kept coming into the house late, she locked all the doors and windows and told all of us "Do

NOT let him in!" Before she did that she had moved all of his things into our cold, dank garage made of cinder block. When he got home late, he got the message and spent the night in the garage. Days later, Mom still did not let him back in the house, and I knew she was testing his will, and she was serious! At one point I was in our basement bathroom having a private moment (a rarity in our house), and he tapped on the window from the outside asking me to let him in. I shook my head no, even though he begged and offered me 50 cents (big money for a kid back in those days). I still stood my ground with another head shake, knowing I would have to contend with Mom if I acquiesced to my big brother's persistent pleas. I just had to leave the bathroom and leave him outside, which I didn't feel good about at that time.

I recall another occasion (after she let him back in the house) when Chico and my Mom were in the kitchen arguing, and the situation was getting pretty heated. It was a battle of the wills again. As their voices got louder and louder, my siblings and I started to gather around her like we had Mom's back, but Chico was still in Mom's face yelling at her as she confidently cooked a huge pot of chili (our dinner) on the stove. His big mistake was to come at her while she was cooking. Just as we were about to intervene before it got too heated, I remember her getting so frustrated with him coming at her like that... so, she quickly hoisted up the pot of chili with pot holders (like the cooking pro that she was) and tossed it onto his chest. He hollered the most curdling scream I had ever heard come for anyone in our house! His immediate reaction after screaming was to quickly run into the only full bathroom we had, which was right next to the kitchen. He jumped in the tub with clothes on trying to wash off and cool down his now burning chest. After that incident, I never saw him get in her face like that *ever* again.

Chico later stopped rebelling against Mom and began to be more constructive and productive, painting and doing yard work around the house to help Mom. He seemed to calm down and get new direction in his late teens and trying to find his way in life. Then he joined the service after high school (following my brother Fran who went into the Navy first straight out of high school). Chico eventually graduated from the Great Lakes Naval Bootcamp, the USO Illinois Great Lakes Naval Center just like Fran did, but a year or so later. He was the leader of his troop during graduation ceremony, swinging his sword so proudly as they marched in at the beginning of the program. It was a long cold trip I took with some of my older siblings to attend, my first long road trip ever. He looked so handsome and in his prime, and I was ever so proud of my big brother in that moment, knowing what he had accomplished and how he had changed so for the positive. He and Fran cursed up a storm in our house; Mom used to stomp on the floor of her bedroom and shout "stop all them MFs down there!" as they would be in the basement playing cards with their neighborhood buddies. But when they returned from the Navy (after graduation and after a deployment overseas), they were much more disciplined stating "yes, ma'am" and "no, sir" quite frequently instead. We all were super proud of both.

In the Navy, Chico learned the trade of cutting hair for the guys (and gals) just like he did for my brothers at home growing up, and that became his trade for life. He has struggled with many demons in his life, but has always been the "Comeback Kid" with his resilience and ability to surmount all his personal challenges. He is now a professional, licensed master barber, who is very artistic with his haircut designs, and with clients lining up at his shop in Cincinnati each and every day. He is the ultimate, driven business man, man of God, and a loving father to his two sons Donovan and Christian. He has been steered awry occasionally, but always gets back up and gets right back to what he was doing, ever so positively committing his life to serving the Lord and giving back to his local Cincinnati community in faith (the east and central district). There he currently runs a ministry and regular weekly food distribution to that community where many look up to him. He is another testament of perseverance through trials in life; he's quite the "trooper" (like the name given to my grandmother "Mother Rob" by Uncle Bill). He is a great contributor to our family *and* to his local community, a great man of God. He has gone through many ups and downs in life, but always remains the optimist, bursting full of personality (and very fashionable too like my Mom). He's the only one of us who can get away with wearing an orange shirt, orange shorts, *and* orange sandals to the cookout while looking like "the Godfather" (which he was called by our

Uncle Bill Adolf Robinson). Chico is one clever brother who is always very sure of himself in all that he does, and I'm so proud of him for that.

"Francis" (We call him "Fran") was/is definitely our family clown and entertainer…. Still is. Every single time you talk to Fran you're bound to laugh and smile! To get a laugh out of us as kids, he would grab and don Mom's scarf and glasses, pull his nose up snout style, and in silly fashion with a cup in hand ask in his deep, gruffy voice (trying to alter it to sound female), "May I please borrow a cup of sugar, Mrs. Kinney?", and he would walk all around the house to make sure we all caught a glimpse of his whimsy. We would just fall apart laughing once that image came around the corner. He would get into a silly, goofy at any time and the surprise of it would come out of nowhere when we least expected it. He was (and still is) just hilarious.

Fran was this tall, lanky, athletic young man who's frame always helped him wear a suit well. He obsessed over making sure that none of his clothes were wrinkled, so he was often pressing some slacks or a shirt before he donned it for public viewing. (Chico did the same, as they often mirrored each other as brothers near the same age.) Fran's combination of fair complexion and huge afro of the times had all the other young ladies in the neighborhood doing a double-take also. I remember he (and Chico) would get a lot of phone calls from girls at our house when they were teens, both attractive young Black men; but to me, they were just my big brothers. I couldn't see that draw to the women yet, but now that I am a woman, I certainly do now.

Both Fran and Chico possess the gift of gab, so they took those phone calls and could be seen snug in a corner of the house, and it would be obvious that they were talking to a girl on the phone.

Fran and Chico both hung pretty tight while we grew up on Grantwood, bonding and growing up together with similar interests and friends. Chico sings beautifully (like my father did), but it was Fran that always found the right words to speak so eloquently, seriously, and thematically... a gift he would develop even more over time into a great ministry. But Fran did *think* he could sing like Barry White with his deep baritone voice. . Before he got so polished with music, and when Barry White came on the radio he would grab a hair brush and sing along to "I'm Never Gonna Give You Up!" He would try to sing that song as if he were the featured artist on Soul Train, while we all would be cracking up laughing. He was truly our family entertainer.

Even into adulthood, Fran absolutely loved music especially after coming back from overseas. He is also the one in my family who taught me the great love of jazz. From traveling abroad, he and Chico brought back hours of reel-to-reel music (popular at the time which held LOTS of music), and would play classic artist for me for the first time like Ronnie Laws, Herb Alpert, Chick Corea, Herbie Hancock, Herbie Mann, and on and on. Sometimes I would play "Sun Goddess" by Ramsey Lewis repeatedly on Fran's new turntable when he would allow me, and listening to this song (with Earth, Wind, and Fire singing background so smoothly) that's when I got a real appreciation for the great jazz compilations that these artists had put together. To this day, this long, mostly instrumental song takes me back to playing records and records in our basement. As I closely examined each album cover to get the details on each artist, I loved doing so while the music played. This is also when I got my first taste of wanting to be a disc jockey (DJ) and to work in radio. Once Chico and Fran showed me how to work their equipment (after I begged them) I would go through their albums meticulously and play all the hits to the delight of everyone in the house upstairs. They would ask, "Is that Nay down there playing the records? She is jamming!" Ever since and into my adulthood, I have been making tapes, CDs, and have been quite versed on various musical artists, but more specifically into (smooth) jazz artists. This love of all kinds of music has definitely transcended from our parents, we are truly the Kids of King (records). I remember so many occasions our dancing in our living room to all the music we played there, Fran positioning the equipment in the living room or dining room, wherever everyone could enjoy it. It was so much fun, everyone dancing, smiling, enjoying our presence together, and everyone taller than me and Carl. And being a family of our size, it was a party with just us alone. But often when our Grantwood neighbors would hear the ruckus from our living room parties, they would knock on the door to join us in the music and dancing fun. Great memories...

As we grew up on Grantwood, I remember my older brother Francis to also be very persuasive with his ways when he wanted something; he could be very convincing. I earned lots of money from braiding his afro (and Chico's too) so that they could maintain their fresh, huge "Jackson Five-like" afros. Carl made a lot of small cash on them too, from running errands and doing tasks assigned by Mom that they did not want to do around the house. A basketball whiz (who thought he was Kareem Abdul-Jabar at the time) Fran, used his tall stature to play basketball often in front of our house or at the local Jonathan Park. He is the one who taught me how to have great form while making a shot, and people are amazed when they see me play basketball, asking me "where did you learn to shoot like that?" It was from big brother Fran, who probably does not even remember teaching this to his little sister. And it was Chico who taught me how to palm the football.

But when we were young, Fran was very mischievous too (often with Chico), but would often get into even more trouble than his older brother (not sure how that was possible, but he unlike "Chico") must have done something that drove my Mom to the brink. He continued to get into trouble at school and in the neighborhood, and Mom feared that he would go in the wrong direction in life (like some other troubled young men in our extended family and in our neighborhood). Mom eventually got tired of it, and she sent *only* Fran away to an all-boys reformatory school called Mount Alverno on the west side of Cincinnati at the young age of 12 (it was like the

"'Boystown' of Cincinnati"). Each week we would visit him as a group after church bringing him Mom's famous home-made peanut butter cookies. But Fran would just cry and plead for Mom to allow him to come home during those visits. Mom would gently hug him, look away, and say "no, baby, not yet". Then she would kiss her defiant son, put all of us back into the car, and then we all would head back to Grantwood without Fran. I think Mom made him an example that none of us should play with her when it came to defiance and discipline telling us all who was *really* in control as a single parent at that time, although she was only 5' 2 inches and 115 lbs. overseeing nine big children. Fran later learned a lot from this, and eventually he gained more respect for Mom and her position. After returning from that place he *never* challenged her again (similar to Chico's chili-on-the-chest incident).

After graduating from the (then) all-boys Purcell Catholic High School in Evanston, he later joined the Navy (before Chico actually), realizing that he should take more of a leadership role in our family). Fran and Chico both would later travel the globe with the Navy, seeing amazing sites, immersing in new cultures, and bringing some of that back home to us to open our eyes to the big world out there. Fran was stationed in the Philippines and Chico in Morocco. They both have gone through quite a metamorphosis in demeanor, life perspective, and discipline in their lives, now with much more positive and influential outcomes.

Fran is now the most gentle and wise brother, husband, father, grandfather, and man of the cloth you would ever meet. He, too, adopted a child (Deneiqua Kinney – now Howard), and has two sons Francois and Stephon "Pop". And yes, Fran still keeps us laughing... a LOT! However, Fran now uses his persuasive powers to impress upon anyone he meets to find a good Bible-based church and stay with the Word of God. Now, when he speaks, the words behind that deep, gruffy voice are wise and deliberate, always affirming and inspiring to those who hear. In a very articulate, demonstrative, and emphatic way, he speaks often of The Good News bringing many souls to Christ. He is a man of great faith now, solely driven by the Word of God (as he had in his role model in this from his big brother Bob). Fran continually guides us/his siblings very closely in faith by leading our weekly Bible study, something we all cling too in these difficult times. He definitely exemplifies his title also given by dear Uncle Bill: "the Governor" of the family.

"Angela" (We call her "Angie" and her middle name "Jewel" is my maternal grandmother's name) eventually in my adulthood became my "road dog", a very close sister, but I could not tell that while we were living at home, probably because of our age difference. Angie was always "very busy" learning and exploring her world which was way too fast for this little sister at the time. I always perceived her as beautiful, on the move, and the one who wanted to stand out in the pack... edgy! She was the daring dreamer in our family that (like her big sister Karen) could see a lot more of the world than we could in our little world of

Evanston in Cincinnati. Angie always had a global mindset, probably from so much reading of all those many romance novels, but I admired how she had such vision. She is one of my fair skinned sisters, and she has aqua blue green eyes with sandy brown hair like mine. As a toddler, she was teased and called my mother's "blue-eyed German child", as her complexion was in contrast to my other siblings. Some genes in our immediate family proved to be both recessive and dominant from both the Kinneys (Daddy's family) and from the Robinsons (Mom's family). Angie definitely had strong genes from the Kinney side of the family, but is built just like a Robinson.

As a teenager, she loved to wear a lot of makeup on those beautiful eyes so that they could bounce right out at you, making them even more prominent on her pretty face. My sister Cecilia used to call her "Sara Mascara", as she would wear a lot of mascara and bat her eyelashes when she received a compliment on them, knowing the uniqueness of those green eyes in our Black community. She was the fashionista among my sisters, making sure her make-up, short skirt, teased afro, and choker necklaces were all in-tact *every time* before leaving the house, and never leaving before doing so... ever! Also, Angie was/is small in stature like Mom, and also just like Mom surprisingly packed with a lot of physical power in spite of her size (so don't ever test that... I've seen some of my siblings and me do it and it wasn't pretty!). Like Mom, many would find out about that physical power when it was too late.

"Ang" got her good looks and strength from my mother Alfreda Kinney, both so very beautiful, and it is consistent with her history on Grantwood. She was also the one who always challenged Mom the most though (similar to Chico and Fran, but the most challenging among the girls in our house). She would try to test her young knowledge, will, and strength on my Mom repeatedly, but could never out clever Alfreda Robinson Kinney. Knowing she needed Mom at the time, she would always announce to my mother during their arguments "As SOON as I turn 18, I am OUT of here!" Committed, she did just that, and she later left our house right after high school graduation, never returning.

I remember an occasion when my Mom, the neighbor Mrs. Brown, and I we were all sitting on the front porch with Mom one summer day, and Angie came prancing out looking all dolled up. Mom asked her, "Where do you think you're going?" Angie put her hand on her "imagination" (I mean her young hip), threw her head back, and said "OUT!" defiantly. Mom calmly said "Really?" There was a moment of silence.... Then suddenly out of nowhere like a flash of lightening, one of the flower pots on the porch ended up smashed against Angie's head and blood started to flow. Angie screamed in disbelief while touching her head and looking at the blood on her hand, "Uh, I'm bleeding!!" Mrs. Brown our neighbor happened to be a registered nurse, and so she took her to the hospital to get her patched up for an act that might be considered child abuse by today's standards. But when asked how she got her injuries, Mom confidently told the doctor "I did it", they patched Angie up, and she quietly came home and healed, slacking off from challenging Mom for a while. I guess they figured: let that child go through her mother's penal system before she ends up in the real one!

Angie always wanted to be and truly was different than all of us, being the "middle child". She obsessively read one Harlequin Romance novel after another, and she was in the "100 books read club" even as a teen. She LOVED reading! She liked flirting and dating a lot, and she reveled in her maturity and changing body as a young woman. She and my other beautiful big sisters would stop traffic wherever we went in public. Angie was a go-getter, a self-starter, and went out on her own to get her first job working at Skyline Chili in Walnut Hills (right down the street from St. Ursula Catholic high school where Karen also attended). She was ground-breaking in getting that job at the well-known chili parlor in Cincinnati working for Kam Misleh and his family (owners at the time who were very nice people to us), and it eventually gave employment as a waitress to all three of her younger sisters subsequently in succession as we all matriculated through high school. I always perceived her as ground-breaking and innovative.

She was also the kind of sister that would answer all the elicit, nasty questions you might have (Like "Why do boys like girls with fat butts?" or "What is it like to kiss a boy?" or "When am I gonna come on MY period like you and Ceal?" or "When do I get to wear a bra?" – that last question they tease me about to this day, now being well-endowed).

Angie would sit me down and talk to me directly and educate me in the most explicit way one-on-one on the lessons
and facts of life. Besides wanting to play in my hair all the
time (she and my other big sisters were often mandated by
Mom to do my hair until I was about nine), she would also
play with my head and joke with me too as I was young and
naïve at the time. One day she pulled me to the side and
whispered, "Nay, did you know that you were adopted? "
My reaction must have told her that I was in disbelief. " Yes,
you and Carl *and* me have been adopted.... Notice we have
green eyes unlike our other brothers and sisters?" After I
thought about it (as a kid) she was right! We DID have different colored eyes and hair from our other siblings. Carl,
Angie, and I are the only ones with green eyes and it was
the first time in my life that I had never realized this! I
went into a panic, and ran screaming and crying to my
mother about it who later cleared up the truth: we all are
blood siblings indeed from the same belly - hers. Angie was
grounded for a week after that little stunt, and got a long
lecture from Mom too about being a responsible big sister
to her younger siblings. But she could get some emotions
stirred up in someone if she wanted/wants to, and she did
that often times with me and Carl (her youngest siblings)
to gauge our reactions as kids. She once convinced me to
cut my shoulder-length hair into a "Farrah Fawcett mullet"
hairdo. When Mom arrived home, she was livid and did
not speak to us directly for a while (and it was hard for her
to look at me without rolling her eyes). I know Mom chose
her battles carefully with her kids to preserve her energy,

but this one seemed like it had her burning up inside, but she has such a cool reaction.

Angie later graduated from the same all-girls high school (St. Ursula Catholic high school) that Kay did, and this is where she confirmed her studies in Spanish which, like me, began at St. Mark in the 8th grade. Always scoring high in academics, very intelligent, she has always been very analytical, calculated, and strategic regarding her next move at anything in life. After Angie's high school graduation, I did not hear from her for a while until more tragedy occurred in our family. She was off studying at Georgetown University. Only second in our family to Bobby, she eventually received a Bachelor's degree from Georgetown University in DC, after having "flown the coop" as she had promised Mom years before. She was ground-breaking in her own way among me and my siblings, taking advantage of every opportunity that came her way academically, and achieving such as a kid coming from a struggling middle-class Black family in Evanston. I admire her greatly for that. She went on to achieve her Master's degree in Library Sciences from the Catholic University of America in Northeast, Washington, D.C. (go figure, being the book nerd from the start). She is now an executive in the federal government, and is a leader in her field.

Later, when I moved to D.C. after I graduated from Central State University in 1985, we got a chance to know each other all over again. During this time (especially when I first arrived in DC and we were both so young) my big sister

"Ang" and I had a BALL in the nation's capital together! I did not get my driver's license until a few years after I arrived in DC, so initially we rode our bikes everywhere since neither of us had a car (this was several waistlines ago for us both). But in DC (like most big cities) you don't really need a car, and so I got to know how to ride the bus and the subway (got lost a few times on the subway). We also hung out at many of the great restaurants (e.g., B. Smith's or the Inn a Little Washington) and night clubs in Washington, D.C. (e.g., RSVP and Hogate's on the waterfront), we went to endless cultural festivals together like the Hispanic Heritage Festival in Adams Morgan (when it was popular to do so), and together we enjoyed many festive events sponsored by our well-to-do employers there in the nation's capital (e.g., annual holiday parties, picnics, and lobster bakes). Angie has guided and mentored me in my child life and in my adult life, always making sure her little sister is on the straight-and-narrow path of goodness in life. That for me has been a true blessing, particularly when I first arrived in DC after college graduation living in a new big, fast-paced city like Washington, D.C. There are certainly many evils to dodge in all big cities (and in the small ones too), but she was determined to do all she could then so that neither of us got caught up in too much mess in "the big city", which is very possible for two attractive young Black females from the Midwest. If we weren't funning on the town taking in the best of DC, we were dashing to visit our brothers Chico and Fran in Norfolk, VA, or taking the train to New York to visit Angie's friend Vivian Scott (now Chew) to see one of the famous acts that she promoted. We've been to Central Park and seen open entertainers there, been entertained in the famous Apollo Theater in Harlem by so many famous acts, and have met many famous musical performers because of "Viv" (even when they would come to DC) making our life in and around DC pretty exciting. And when our people would visit from out-of-town, they loved "seeing all the Black professional people" along with so many other cultures, and my big sister was there to show me all that was new, great, and interesting in the nation's capital. She was always so keen to impress upon me the importance of managing my physical image (like Cindy did when I was younger) and about networking and positioning to get the most prestige and enjoyment out of my life personally and professionally. She took me shopping to get my very first business suit (I'll never forget that and how much care she took to make sure I would look my best). To have such support in my young and adult life, and from my precious big sister, was (is) priceless.

She is single with no kids, is a two-time breast cancer survivor, something that was a challenging time for her I know (but it was for me also). At first, she did not want to involve me, and did not want me to go with her to see the doctor. I remember breaking down crying with her and asking "Please, Angie, let me go with you to the appointment to see your doctor!" And she eventually gave in, and she allowed me to go with her to see and talk with her doctor about her prognosis and her anticipated treatments. The second round she experienced, I also remember being right in the middle of breast feeding my newly born infant while she was going through additional surgeries, something I actually felt guilty about at the time. They were cutting into her (but to save her life), while I was pouring out life (milk) from my breasts into my daughter Julia.

Working as a hospital administrator at the time, our hospital always sponsored a team for the "Race for the Cure" national race/walk to raise funds for breast cancer research. I remember the first time I invited Angie to come down and walk with me and our team, and we walked down on the national mall from her house (which was then close by in the Capitol Hill neighborhood). As we approached the mall and we saw all the pink (knowing so many others and their loved ones were tackling breast cancer too), we were overcome with emotion and had to stop and just hug each other and cry at what she had accomplished in battling this disease. It was a moment I'll never forget, spent on the National Mall with my precious big sister whom I thought, at one point, that I might possibly lose. And, once we did approach the crowd to register to walk, to see all the tributes of those who did NOT win the battle pinned to the backs of those walking was just heart-breaking and gave us both even more resolve to walk for everyone tackling breast cancer... it sucks! Angie had to go down a very difficult path (physically and mentally) that I don't know how I could have possibly navigated, but she did it, with Alfreda Robinson Kinney strength... *and* she did it twice!!

Still in the DC area in VA, not on Capitol Hill anymore, she is now living her best life very comfortably, knowing the freedoms and the opportunities that DC has brought her, and she has brought me into that perspective now too. I am immensely proud of her, all the obstacles she has hurdled, her many academic and professional accomplishments in life, and especially her ability to speak FOUR languages! (English, Spanish, French, Italian) She is incredibly smart and clever (again just like her Mom), and she is the only one among us all with an advanced degree. But she is still the humble, helpful, giving person at heart that we were all raised to be... just now, a lot wiser at life, it's slings and arrows. Her name among the siblings is "Jiggs" (again as defined by our always "mackin' spodie" - well-dressed - Uncle Bill).

"Cecilia" (her nickname is "Ceal") was an intimidator (at least to her younger siblings) when we were growing up, but looking at her now, you'd hardly know it as she is quite the compassionate and empathetic soul. Although, to this day, she will always challenge you, making her opinion known to all (courteously) in her deep gruffy voice. Her voice is so deep that over the phone, she is often mistaken as a man. Another very fair-skinned beautiful sister, Ceal has long coal black hair (dark hair features like my father) with beautiful chestnut brown eyes, and her birthday falls right between my mother and fathers "smack dab" in the middle of July. She was rough with her younger siblings, mandating and challenging us around the house at every opportunity. She and "Ang" hung together often, being just a year apart. I found that as a child in a big family, you ended up "pairing up" often with just one other sibling to kind of "tag-team" life in our house. (It was Karen and Bobby, Chico and Fran, me and Carl, etc., and it was definitely Ceal and Angie.) They both got into fights with each other sometimes (over something that wasn't shared fairly in our house, a common argument there), but they also had occasional run-ins with the other neighborhood girls, often due to jealousy or cliques. They would end up in some scuffles, and would come home looking kind of roughed up. Me and my other fair-skinned siblings got some flak from neighborhood kids over our appearance (being light-skinned with unique eye colors) and Angela and Cecilia surely held those features, so they stood out from most of the neighborhood girls in particular. But the neighborhood girls didn't realize that with four brothers teaching them how to be rough and strong, the neighborhood girls did not stand a chance. So, we had battles among one another, but also skirmishes with kids in the neighborhood, but the Kinney kids always stood their ground in each melee.

At home on Grantwood, Ceal (and all my older siblings) would demand certain things of her younger siblings that made life convenient for her (them), because she (they) could. She knew that Cindy was meticulous about doing laundry and pressing our uniform clothes in preparation for school. Once she stole one of the few clean, well-pressed white butterfly-collar blouses that Cindy had carefully prepared, leaving Cindy fuming. And they would argue over that regularly. Ceal (and our other siblings did this too) often sending Carl and I to the store to retrieve whatever goodies she (they) wanted from there, and we were frequent gophers to get things around the house for everybody, parents and "Mother Rob" (my grandmother) included. One day my brother Fran noticed what he thought was abusive behavior by Ceal toward Carl, and Fran told Carl "come here... I've got something to tell you." We were all down in the basement away from my mother when Fran (who also competed with Ceal often) whispered into Carl's ear, "I'll give you fifty cents if you go up and just bust Ceal right in the face... *right now*!" Well-motivated by the thought of what fifty cents could buy us at the local Blair Market corner store which we frequented, and always trustingly following his big brother's command, Carl proceeded to walk right up to Ceal and he punched her square in the middle of her face. She reeled in shock as she fell back from the power of Carl's well-motivated blow to the face. And we all stood there in amazement for a minute that Carl had just decked the person who always bullied us (David had conquered Goliath!). And Fran burst out hollering in delight, congratulating Carl for the feat he has just done. But in turn, Fran and Chico had to quickly hold back an angry Ceal who began to "windmill" on Carl, and she was about to trounce him bad in turn! They eventually got the situation under control, and got her flared temper to calm down before Mom could notice what was occurring in the basement. But it was a memorable moment in our childhood that we still laugh about to this day. Fran could surely be an instigator too!

When she wanted to go somewhere, Ceal, like Angie, would have a fit when Mom would say "take your little sister with you" (meaning me), and they would jump up and down in a tantrum in protest. I knew they loved me, but in these moments, I knew it was really Mom wanting to give them a little "tracking device" when they went out in the form on a tattling little sister who often did just that. It would drive my siblings crazy how I would give my mother a full report on everything that I observed around the house. When Angie and Ceal would be experimenting with cigarettes in our upstairs walk-in closet, as soon as they knew that I knew, Mom would eventually know too, and then they surely would be in trouble. They probably all watched what they did around me, but I saw it as nothing but loyalty and helpful in being the ultimate informant for my Mom, who already had so many challenges managing all of us. At the time, I saw it as being on her side and a great support for her.

Ceal and Angie also led the interesting fun events among us younger kids around the house like birthday parties, when our cousins visited for sleepovers - our many nights of sleeping on the front porch in the summer, or playing hide and go seek in the house one of the few times when Mom left the house to just us. We would cut all the lights out in the house, and Ceal or one of my other sisters would guide me and Carl (the youngest) to hide, often together, telling us to stay there quietly until we were found (and we would patiently wait until found by one of our siblings, a point of shear elation for Carl and I). Ceal and Angie would (especially when our cousins were over) would play records in the basement, and we all would join in line dancing to songs like "I Don't Wanna Lose Your Love" by the Emotions and to Grover Washington's "Mister Magic" (two of Fran's albums, I think). I even remember when Ceal, Angie, and my cousin Levie orchestrated a perfume fight among all of us (obviously when Mom was away... she would have never approved of us wasting her Avon's Sweet Honesty and Jean Nate body splash on one another!).

Ceal led us in some fun activities at home, but she also demonstrated an awesome work ethic and strong need for cleanliness (probably learned from both of my parents). Ceal and Angie got jobs at Skyline Chili at the same time, but Angie went off to college shortly after that. Ceal continued to diligently show up for work at Skyline always on time for her shift even though she had to catch a city bus to get there. When Ceal left Skyline to take on another job, she convinced the demanding but wise and kind Adib Misleh (owner at the time, but his son Kam Misleh is the owner to this day) that her position should go to Cindy, her little sister. Next, she got me a job there, her youngest sister. This left Cindy and me as the only Kinney sisters to remain working at Skyline at the time, but before that it was a blissful time working with my big sisters, as I started feeling like an adult having my own job. Before Ceal left Skyline, she trained Cindy and I on a lot of necessary tasks to work there efficiently, and how to ward off the many hungry-eyed men coming through to get not only chili, but possibly a date. She and Angie taught me how to react when men are approaching you, flirting with you. Many would ask "Can I go?", and they would both blush and state every so pleasantly "No, thanks" while maintaining the guy's dignity. All my sisters displayed such elegance, style, and feminine charm (like Mom), but Ceal specifically was strong in work ethic. She (like my other sisters) definitely demonstrated that you must get up, get out, get busy, and stay productive with work and the various tasks of a woman and mother each day of your life in order to survive and live well.

Always a hard worker, after graduating high school, Ceal worked in the local United Dairy Farmer (UDF) stores common to Cincinnati that sell some of the best ice cream – butter pecan (short of Graeter's ice cream, a well-known German ice cream maker in Cincinnati that has the ice cream of the gods). She went on to work at the University of Cincinnati, and ended up working there for over 30 years. While at UDF, she helped raise me as I was just finishing high school, and she was instrumental in caring for me, feeding me, being a confidant, and helping me navigate my (our) grief. She gave me a place to stay while finishing high school, as I matriculated through college, and as I studied abroad in Mexico, a very critical time in my life. My daughter Julia bears her name (Julia Cecilia).

When I finished college, she would visit Angie and me (and Fran and Chico in Norfolk) on the east coast in the summers, and we would go clubbing together (sometimes Cindy would join us too). Once Ceal, Angie, and I met with our brothers in Norfolk for a weekend of beach time and clubbing, and we had rented a car to get back from the beach to the hotel, to their apartments, and to the clubs in the evening. The night on the way back from the club, Ceal was driving, and it was close to 2am. We were taking the main two-lane highway back to the hotel from the club, and there was almost no one on the road at that hour. But ahead of us we saw headlights, and we were on a road where there was a concrete barrier between the eastbound and westbound traffic. We were heading eastbound, and someone was on our side of the highway driving the wrong way toward us! Once me and my sisters realized what was occurring, we all started shouting for Ceal to "pull the car over to the side of the road!" to let that person going the wrong way bypass us. Ceal did so quickly, and we waited for the car to pass us, and it did so at top speed... *going the wrong way*. We sat there in the car and prayed asking God to give that person safe passage to home and not take a life, for ours had been spared that night. We hugged each other, and Ceal carefully drove us back to the hotel, all of us being on full alert that we had fatefully just escaped death. I am always eternally grateful to my sister for her quick thinking and calm during that situation to bring us to safety. She has always been one to warn me about dangers in life and precautions to take to live a good life (like many of my siblings). To have this repeated support and guidance from various loving siblings like Ceal is something that many are not blessed with in life, and I never take this for granted. Ceal was there and present for me at a very critical, confusing, and sad time in my young life, right when I was grieving heavily from my Mom's death and realizing that I was an orphan... it was depressing. But she helped me make the decisions that I needed to make in order to proceed onto a productive and promising adulthood.

Ceal, always the head of household, has provided for me as a mother too. But she has also raised her three children often solo (Chivon, Brittany, and Demetrius "Dink"), and now has many grandchildren to share life with as well. As she matured and experienced life's slings and arrows, she has become a gentler and more patient spirit toward all of her family members, but still was/is always good about making her point known among the crowd. *(I guess we all got this skill from yelling over one another as we grew up.)* She, ironically, became a lot like my mother: domesticated and focused on maintaining every aspect of our/her home and family. She has since retired, and her home is often the center of many of our family gatherings over the years. Now a matriarch of her own family, she is still truly focused on being the rock of her/our home and family in all ways.

"Cynthia" (We call her "Cindy") and she was/is the ultimate domestic goddess as we were growing up. I swear, she wanted to be just like Mom! But that was ok with me, because Mom was way too busy with so many other matters it seems that Cindy made sure all my needs were met... I found great comfort in that, and I thank my sister Cindy to this day for that. I did NOT like to bathe, being the tomboy, that I was. Cindy made sure that I bathed regularly and that all of my uniform clothes were well pressed (until she taught me how to do them for myself). She also taught me a lot about female etiquette, something it seemed like my other sisters figured I'd just fall into. My Mom was pretty good about educating me on that too. But I was closer to Cindy each day as she put on her bras, etc. and took care of herself personally. I observed both she and Mom a LOT in how they cared for their femininity. I always saw them as meticulous with that: cleanliness and looking/acting like a lady. She truly taught me the finer points of my womanhood, but she was also very athletic and sporty and kept me on my toes physically. She is the only one on the planet that could possibly convince me to jog with her from Grantwood to Eden Park in Cincinnati and back (about 6 miles). This definitely was several waistlines ago for us both, but she still jogs everywhere! I admire her for her constant focus on her health, fitness, personal, and spiritual well-being. She is a great role model for me in that regard.

She and I (and other sisters before us) played volleyball at St. Mark. The very athletic Sr. Rosemary Kelly there would make us practice often, leading our team to victory in many matches. But we did lose a few, so in that I learned a great lesson in life. Either way, Sr. Kelly was always there to guide us whether we won or not. There were occasions when we had matches with the teams of other Cincinnati Catholic grade schools (predominantly white), and when we did win they would try to make us feel bad... prejudice raising its ugly head again, and instead of showing sportsmanship and congratulating us, we would receive shouts of "Nigger go home!" as we went back to our school bus that transported us there, Sr. Kelly keeping an eye out to make sure nothing unnecessary would erupt among our two competing teams. You are supposed to be coached that at the end of each game both teams do walk in a line next to the other tapping hands with everyone whether you won or lost to show good sportsmanship. Some teams would not want to come and do a "team tap" with us at all at the end of the game, and we kept walking with our win. Knowing what we all had just encountered, Sr. Kelly, ever-encouraging of our spirits, would get us on the bus, and on the way would lead us in a rousing rendition of Steam's 1969 hit: "Na Na Hey Hey (Kiss Him) Goodbye!", singing that chorus repeatedly until our bus was out of earshot, much to the chagrin of the other sore losing team. Everyone at St. Mark always made us feel like true victors regardless of our circumstances. Cindy and her besties Stephanie Mayfield and Tammy Daniels were often with us on those trips. We didn't know it then, but these experiences with our St. Mark buddies would bond us for years to come.

But Cindy and I both found solace in volleyball, often when it was just us two which was great. We kept a ball of some sort around our house using it as a volleyball until Mom noticed our talent and bought one for us one Christmas. As a young girl, if I didn't go to nearby Jonathan Park with Deneen to play tetherball (of which I was an expert second only to "Nina"), I was going there with Cindy to bump our volleyball around. Cindy and I would go to the park to avoid Mom's complaints about the possibility of the ball hitting one of her windows which with nine kids had occurred a time or two, especially from her sons. She and I, in deep concentration, would hit the ball in the air volleying it between us, sometimes keeping it off the ground for up to 30 minutes to our amazement. And when we teamed up in the kitchen, we were a great assist to Mom who had to prepare food for all of us. Cindy proudly took over this role of cooking meals for us to ease Mom's long list of tasks, so you often found Cindy in the kitchen making pancakes or baking her delicious toll house chocolate chip cookies (like the ones that Bobby tried to rob when he stopped by the house after work on that fateful day). And me wanting to be ever-pleasing to my Mom also, I would assist Cindy closely in the kitchen to prepare meals for our family.

Cindy would often be in charge of cooking breakfast for everyone (especially when our Robinson cousins came over – Diane and David or Rocky/Raymond and Lisa). Diane and David were born 2 of eleven children to my mother's bother Gus (Charles) Robinson and his wife Aunt Mary. They lived on the lower west side of Cincinnati while Lisa and Rocky, kids of my mother's brother Ray, lived north of town in the more affluent College Hill community in Cincinnati. Our Aunt Mabel's (my Dad's sister) kids Chris, Levie, and Darrell stayed with us often, but actually lived with their Mom on Burnet Avenue in Avondale. We never cared what our cousins had or where they lived; we were just ecstatic when they (Kinneys or Robinsons) would visit us and stay overnight. And Cindy often led the charge of caring for the "extra kids" to ease Mom's load.

From working domestically alongside Mom, Cindy picked up her skills and sometimes mandated me to do so when I was not always so motivated. This is where I picked up my current automatic need to tidy up everything around the house, the need to do laundry weekly like clockwork, and to think in the morning about "what are we having for dinner?". I really wanted to be a tomboy and run after my brother Carl (just a year older than me), trying to copy his every move. But Cindy would curtail that action from time to time. When I first started at St. Mark in first grade, it was Cindy who called me in, showed me how to press my Catholic school uniform and butterfly collar blouses to prepare for school the night before. She is the one who directly cared for me, *mandating* me to bathe when I did not want to (and sometimes standing there to make sure I did it right), making sure I did all of my chores around the house, and keeping me safe and directly protective of me (and Carl) from the challenges of my older siblings. Looking back, Cindy was the one I was with most often to care for my daily personal needs as a very young girl (probably while Mom was still grieving Daddy's death). All of my sisters helped me develop properly into the budding young woman that I was becoming at the time, but Cindy closely "mothered" me consistently, daily, and throughout the day.

At one point in our teen years, she joined me to attend high school at Ursuline Academy of Cincinnati since her high school in nearby Norwood (Regina Catholic High School) would close like many Catholic parishes in Cincinnati due to scandal in the Catholic church. Many Catholic families in Cincinnati were leaving the church and schools, sending families (and students like Cindy and her besties) to other Catholic schools in the area forcing parishes to merge. So, in her junior year, she joined me at Ursuline Academy where I had won a scholarship. I remember Mom telling her "you're going with your sister to Ursuline", a deal already brokered by my high school Principal (Sr. Rose Helene Wildehaus... I later found out she made sure that all of us St. Mark girls ended up at that elite all-girls school in the Blue Ash section of Cincinnati. A major event was about to change our lives; we experienced it during this time *together* while in high school and while working together at Skyline Chili (where she taught me even more about cooking and food prep). Cindy attended UA her junior and senior year of high school, then graduated (accepting to attend Bluffton College between Lima and Findlay, Ohio and Lake Erie). I was a freshman and sophomore while she was there. Once she left Ursuline, I felt alone during my junior year without here there. By the end of my junior year at UA and her freshman year in college we would both experience a life-changing event that would bring us even closer together as sisters than we already were.

Of all my sisters, Mom put Cindy and Ceal in a dance troupe around 1972, and again Mom said to them "take your little sister with you", and just like that I was part of this group of limber beautiful young Black women (my two sisters included) who presented our talents at local schools during various dance recitals. Mom received the recommendation from Mrs. Allison who also attended St. Mark. Her daughter Tina was also part of the dance troupe, so we knew some of the girls from school. Fond are the memories I have of us waking up Saturday mornings to take the long walk to a building on Clarion in Evanston to practice. Afterwards we would hand-wash our leotards to avoid washing a full load of clothes (something Cindy made sure I did alongside her after each Saturday practice). Then we would leave them to air-dry in our common bathroom much to the complaints of my brothers who had to stare at them as they stood up taking a tinkle. Our troupe danced to modern jazz and some current R&B slow songs. I had to do a dance with some other younger girls in the group to Diana Ross' "Touch Me in the Morning", and now when I hear that song it brings back great memories of our time dancing together as sisters.

When we first joined the troupe, Cindy was a bit of a nerd in appearance, but cute as a button, looking just like our late Uncle Arliss Robinson in the face, which brought her much love and affection from our grandmother "Mother Rob" who missed him dearly. (I would later learn that dear Uncle Arliss died of lockjaw at the young age of 17. Since Cindy looked so much like him, she would often longingly call her "Little Arliss"). Looking back, she seemed like the cute, nerdy little kid who wore blue kitty cat shaped eyeglasses that were often broken. And to add to their appeal, they were often mended with masking tape along one hinge or another (or both). Sometimes it was not in the budget to afford an immediate fix of her much-needed spectacles.

Cindy was always the proper one to always follow the rules, and to stay on task with everything required of her in the house. She was not only my big-sister and close care-giver, but she was my disciplinarian too. She never whooped me, but would give me stern warnings as to what to do and what not to do. And I know when she would use my whole name: "Naomi Kinney, you must not....", I knew she meant business and to take heed intently. She was one for keeping particularly Carl and me safe, but once she got into a bit of a predicament. One Saturday, Chico wanted to go to Twin Fair (nearby shopping center in Norwood about one mile away) to buy something he needed, and Mom said "take someone with you". None of the older kids wanted to go, so Cindy, Carl, and I tagged along with Chico. To avoid any potential confrontations on Montgomery Road in Norwood, sometimes we would cut through the railroad tracks behind Xavier University to get there (something city officials even advised against, but we were in a group and so felt safe together). We got what we needed and some snacks for on the way back, and began to head back by way of the railroad tracks behind the store on this hot summer day. We got about mid-way home on the tracks, and Chico forgot dishwashing liquid that he was supposed to get at the store for Mom. He did not want to arrive at home with our four bags in tow and not have what she had asked for. So, he announced "Hey, we gotta go back and get the dishwashing liquid for Mom, or she's gonna be mad at me!" Cindy protested and did not want to go; she was too hot and tired. So, after trying to get her to go back with us, Chico told her, "OK, just sit here on this box with these bags and we'll be right back. Do NOT move, and do NOT talk to any strangers!" Carl and I went with Chico back to the A&P in the Twin Fair shopping center to get what Mom had asked for. When we returned, we could see far in the distance, Cindy tied to the switchbox, bags missing from her side and she was yelling for us. Once he recognized what was happening, Chico dropped everything and took off running toward Cindy like the football player he was in order to rescue his little sister, carefully crossing Dana Avenue as he did. Carl and I eventually caught up with Chico, and he had taken the twine off that secured her hands to the switchbox, and was cursing at what looked like two white guys (railroad bums) running down the railroad tracks toward Tadpole Pond with all the stuff we had just purchased. We could see them laughing and giving us the finger, and were incredibly angry at what they did to our sister. But we were glad that she was safe and unharmed... just scared to death. Once we got home and told Mom what had happened, she forbade us to go through the railroad tracks, and we frequented there less and less, knowing the dangers that lurked there for young Black kids. Ever since, Cindy always stuck with the group and played it even more safe and cautious in life.

Cindy grew tall very fast all of a sudden, and she had huge feet that grew with her very long legs for her body, perfect for balancing on when we received our ballet shoes in our dance troupe. Then one day when we held a recital at then Parham Elementary school also in Evanston, Cindy performed a solo in those big pink ballet shoes to Stevie Wonder's "You and I", and I was simply stunned at the beauty and poise that my sister Cindy displayed during that performance looking like an elegant swan blossoming right before me!! At the end of the song, when Stevie repeatedly sings "You and I", she continuously did pirouettes around the stage to each round of "You and I". I was just mesmerized and SO very proud that this was MY sister dancing across the stage on her own with such grace and poise! Wow! I have even more fond dance troupe memories of her out-performing all the other girls in the troupe; they knew she was the best in the troupe! But in this moment particularly, still visualizing her performing like so, such a demonstration of strength in posture, and physical endurance... it still makes me emotional and sends chills up my spine whenever I hear that song now. She was truly an amazing ballet dancer.

Cindy eventually blossomed into an absolute FOX, wearing her makeup to precision, and realizing more and more every day the power of her maturing figure, often stopping traffic everywhere we went. Her long lanky light brown, athletic frame (excellent combination of Robinson and Kinney blood) turned into smooth feminine physically-fit curves. When we went to the swimming pool with Cindy and she would wear a bikini, the guys would lose control and be hanging all around us with stupid expressions on their faces, trying to get her attention. It was a new and interesting spectacle for me to observe: my big sister who was once so meek and modest and seemingly not very attractive growing up, now getting *so* much attention for her stunning and flattering feminine features that had developed on her now gorgeous frame. As a little sister, I always wanted to be like her in her elegance and beauty, in her discipline and commitment to being healthy, in her domestic abilities, and in her joyful spirit. She doesn't even know how beautiful she was/is *(inside and out, then and now)*.

After attending Bluffton College, Cindy later returned to Cincinnati for a bit, working in healthcare with medical records. She eventually found new love and moved to Tennessee to start a new family there. She now has two grown sons (Gabriel and Jeremi) and a daughter (Ebonee). She is now a grandmother, a true domesticate, and family woman (a lot like Mom). She is also a spirited sister of great faith. Faith, family, and home (in that order) have always been major priorities for her in her life now and always will be. Cindy is still the same fun-loving, funny guide and mentor that she's always been throughout my life. As a kid sometimes called "Mr. Magoo" by Fran for her glasses and "Arliss" for her facial features, she still stops traffic *(all my sisters do, really)*.

"Carl" had a few nicknames; one created by Ceal was "Big `n Yella" from the cartoon cowboy on the 70s Sugar Pops commercial, all because of his tall height and fair skin (we eventually shortened it to "Big Yell"). As a kid, he was my hanging buddy and play pal growing up on Grantwood. Being the two youngest, everyone looked after the two of us very closely, and we received a lot of love, care, and guidance from our older siblings, often two at a time *together*. Carl and I were a tag-team, and could often be found running around the house after one another. I followed him everywhere, and I think he liked the fact that he had one sibling younger than him under his daily influence, instead of his older siblings who always told him what to do. And I would take on every dare he threw my way. He used to flip his eyelids so that you could see the red under his lid, and I would try to mimic this, but Mom would put us "in the corner" if she caught us doing so after warning us to "stop doing that!"

Often mistaken as twins, Carl and I had the same light-brown hair with blond hair glowing fuzz on the edge of our hairline and on our cheeks. Only born a year apart, and being outside on our bikes as often as possible, our light-colored hair (Angie's too) only got brighter throughout the summer months, and we were reminded often of how we looked alike by our friends and neighbors. All of us had that "summer glow" (my Mom especially once she got summer sun), but in the winter, our hair darkened and our skin became pale. Carl and I went everywhere together on our bikes when we were young. We sang silly songs together, often those from summer camp or from St. Mark (like "Dem Bones Gonna Rise Again" – a cute Easter song we learned from Mrs. Burke about Jesus' Resurrection). But Carl and I also got into trouble together. When I talked about "the pairing" of siblings, he and I were quite the pair growing up, and I wanted to do everything that he did (even as a girl) which often proved impossible. But I would still try!

Those were the days when we could ride our bikes around the block without shoes on without worry about our feet getting torn up. Carl was always VERY intelligent and skilled with his hands. He often would take things apart and would put them back together again, like his model airplanes that filled the dining room table. Carl and I were serious explorers around my house, often running up through the laundry chute that led from the first-floor bathroom to the basement. We had rats that ran through our neighborhood, especially on trash day, but we always considered them pretty harmless, being too young to know their real danger. The little, baby rats were particularly cute, we thought. On one particular hot, summer day in July, Carl found one and caught it. One of our neighbors Shelby Jackson, who was a few years older than Carl, convinced him to take it home. It happened to be mom's birthday (July 15th) and Carl thought "let's give Mom one of these cute little creatures for her birthday!" So, he and I proceeded to the back-screen door both proudly thinking this was a great idea, Carl holding the little baby rat in hand that we thought was just adorable. Carl yelled for Mom to come to the back door and she did, poking her head out the back door to give us a once over. Carl pushed the cute little rat up to mom's face and proudly announced "Happy Birthday, mom!" In total fear and shock, Mom slapped the rat out of Carl's hand like a baseball bat to a ball, and hit it so hard that it smacked against the back-porch wall and dropped dead to the floor immediately. We both stood there shocked, sad (for the cute baby rat), and confused at what she had just done. Then out of nowhere, she quickly grabbed both of us by the front of our shirts (at the same time) and dragged us to the bathroom immediately for a *very* hot bath (this is when we were young enough to bathe together). We sadly sat in that tub full of hot water then, sulking and confused about what just happened, and after this incident, our siblings did not want to touch us for a while, thinking we had rabies or something. We all laugh about this story to this day with them always saying "YOU and Carl!" shaking their heads. We have many other stories like this where we were always getting into something *together*, one being triggered or dared by the other to get into this or that.

Once the boys got a chemistry set for Christmas (which Mom NEVER did again after all the experiments they did), but I remember Carl grabbing the chemistry set one day and telling me "I bet we can get these test tubes to bubble over with the liquid soap in the kitchen!" I didn't know exactly what he meant then, but I ran after him to the kitchen where he proceeded to put some dishwashing liquid in one of the test tubes, turned on the top burner to the stove, and he held the test tube over the burner on the stove holding it with an oven mitt to avoid getting burned. Suddenly balls of bubbles (soap) began to shoot out of the test tube in reaction to the heat and each blob of soapy projectile hit the adjacent wall in the kitchen. After the first shot realizing the fun miracle of science we had just discovered, we stood there for a moment looking at each other with our eyes widened with excitement. Ready for more excitement, he put the test tube back over the burner to have it go again, while I loaded another test tube with liquid soap to keep on deck for when this one ran out. I would keep Carl's artillery going so the fun soapy mess could continue in the kitchen. Once we had gone through two test tubes of soap and enough soapiness covered the wall, Carl said "All right, we gotta stop and clean up before Mom sees this! But at least it's clean!" And we laughed while we quickly cleaned up the mess *together* (we cleaned up a lot of our messes together often before anyone else in the house got to see what we were up to).

When we learned our way to St. Mark regularly on our own, Mom gave us more freedom to move about the neighborhood, but encouraged Carl to "look after your little sister." One Saturday evening, Carl and I wanted to go to Saturday afternoon mass (to avoid having to get up early on Sunday morning to go then – good Catholics went to church once a week religiously). One particularly cold, winter Saturday with no snow on the ground, Mom allowed us to go, but bundled us up well before we made the three-block walk to get to the beautiful St. Mark Church campus, the same path we took to school each day. This evening, it was dusk (still some light in the sky), and Carl and I approached Montgomery Road right in front of Aunt Chick's building, and attempted to cross. Carl made a dash and said "Come on!" and like I always had done without thinking I ran after my brother and followed his command, and then I heard and felt a THUD!... and then the lights went out for me. I woke up in front of St. Mark on the ground with blood covering my face and a stranger holding me telling me to "hold on little one!" I kept spitting blood not sure what had just happened, and I did not see Carl around. I had been hit by a car that threw me fifty feet onto one of the cement pylons in front of the church. I later found out that my loyal brother Carl who, after getting me settled with an adult on the side of the road, immediately took off running home to get Mom who appeared minutes later (I remember) in a night gown and housecoat in the middle of winter on Montgomery Road crying hysterically "My baby, my baby!!" That was the last thing I remember before waking up in Cincinnati Children's Hospital with a concussion on my forehead (the origin of all the blood that was covering my face after the accident). The doctor later told my Mom that "your daughter's hood and thick pony tails/hair saved her from multiple contusions... it probably saved her life". And Mom later told me that "it was good that your brother was there with you when that happened. He ran all the way home like lightening that day to let us know what was going on." She also let me know that when she went to make a payment on my hospital bill that she discovered it had been paid in full. The nervous man who hit me (I only faintly remember him, dark-haired thin Caucasian older man) had paid it off. Carl said he was a taxi driver. Whoever that angel was, thank you. (Praise God!)

A memory that I will forever be etched in my mind is when I arrived home from Children's Hospital after the accident. That day Mom and I arrived home from the hospital with the assistance of Mrs. Brown our next-door neighbor who was also a nurse. Mom relied on her often for assistance with our bumps and scrapes and she had a car at the time. She always obliged, being good friends; we would often find them out on our front porch just talking and talking over iced tea. But this day when we all three entered our house, all my siblings were laying across Mom's bed (the only bedroom on the first floor of Grantwood) watching the only television set in the house, entranced in some program that was on the TV, probably Barnabas Collins in "Dark Shadows", a show Carl and I were not allowed to watch. When I walked in and said "hey!" they all turned around and started hugging and kissing on me… a moment etched in my mind forever. The outpouring of love from all of them, all at once was just euphoric. Here, I thought I was the tag-along head-ache of a little sister, but they *really* loved me and I definitely felt it that day (the whole day)! In this house so full of kids and with such limited space, they actually missed me the past two weeks! I'm telling you, when I'm sick and on my deathbed thinking of all the good thoughts of my life, this will definitely be a go-to flashback on which I will rely. Mom and Mrs. Brown also held three shopping bags of toys that I had accumulated from various guest visitors and nurses during my two-week stay at the hospital, with my head still bandaged over my face from the concussion I had sustained. I was already closely-monitored as one of the youngest in our family, but after this event everybody kept a very close eye on my daily activities. It was ok with me; it just meant getting more sibling love.

*****

Evanston used to be a predominantly white Irish/German community, and this was one of the reasons why the Archdiocese of Cincinnati agreed to invest in giving the green light to build the beautiful historic structure of St. Mark Catholic Church there on Montgomery Road back in 1905, a church parish originally dedicated to the Missionaries of the Precious Blood. The property owner was a Mary Klinckhamer, and she donated the property cornerstone which later became the church and school. A convent was added in 1909 to accommodate the Sisters of the Precious Blood who ran the school. When the school and the church hit capacity in 1911 due to the growing middle-class of Irish/German Catholics filling the neighborhood, they decided to build a bigger church structure that would house up to 800 people. Henry Schlacks was recruited as an architect, having designed previous buildings at Notre Dame and Xavier University campuses. Additionally, Joseph G. Steinkamp & Brothers served as an associate architectural firm at the time. The cornerstone was laid in 1914, and the historic church was built modeling the pattern of the Basilica of Santa Maria in Trastavere in Cosmedin, Italy. It is brown brick and terracotta exterior with a Verona façade, a roof adorned with Roman orange ceramic tiles, and a 130-foot campanile (a free-standing bell tower). The spacious interior includes two chapels, a gallery for the choir, and a huge altar that contains beautiful images of the 12 apostles. In 1922 the school burned down, but was immediately replaced the following year, adding in several improvements to the facility and campus. A huge pipe organ was built into the back of the church in 1933, and in the 40s, a bowling alley and a youth club were added to the church. Then in 1950, a rectory was built on the grounds of where the old church was, and this became a residence for the pastors and priests (and also had meeting rooms for parish business). There were many German and Irish families in attendance at the school and church, including a not-so-famous Doris Kappelhoff (who later became singer/actress "Doris Day"). There was a rumor that they had the desk on which she scribbled her name in storage in the annals of the school. There are many stories told about the historic St. Mark parish including the book "Forbidden Love" by Lisa Jones Gentry that told of a clandestine relationship between a priest (Fr. William Grau and Sr. Sophie Legocki). It obviously was a very close-knit community in many ways among the brothers and sisters of the Precious Blood who resided there.

In the late 1960s, many white families began to leave Evanston, and middle-class Black families moved into the community, keeping it clean and pristine (as I remember growing up). I remember seeing many white classmates when I was young, but almost none by the time I graduated. But for the Black families that had move into Evanston in the 60s, this was a wonderful, ideal family-oriented location in which our (my) parents decided to raise us. Carl and I (and all my siblings) ran this neighborhood freely and safely... as long as we did not cross the railroad tracks into Norwood by ourselves. Besides attending school at St. Mark, many of us sang in the church choir, were in youth groups, and participated in many other aspects of being parishioners of St. Mark. And many of my brothers served in the church as altar boys, but I think Carl served in that capacity for the longest time among all my brothers.

This was also the time when construction began on interstate Highway I-71 *(refer to map insert at the beginning of the book)* running northeast to southwest across Cincinnati's "east side" and ending at the "Norwood Lateral" – a stretch of inter-city highway that connected I-71 to I-75, another major highway that runs from Michigan to Florida (I found growing up and confirmed as an adult that there was always a rift between the "east side" and the "west side" of Cincinnati due to class and heritage – German and Irish.) I-71 would connect Cincinnatians to Columbus Ohio more directly and efficiently. So, the construction began, and it sliced directly through the Evanston community affecting many families who were also parishioners of the nearby St. Mark Church. The highway runs directly against the backyard of the church and the convent house (saved then by this community redevelopment project). I'm sure it disrupted many other communities (black and white) as well throughout Cincinnati at that time. As the construction was under way, Carl and I were in our single digits and were young explorers of our neighbor-hood, and we felt safe doing so, but we still liked a little adventure every now and then. Mom would be emphatic in repeatedly warning us "Do NOT play in that construction site!", which was located just two blocks from our house on Woodburn. Woodburn Avenue was cut off between Jonathan and Brewster (the location of King Records) and on the way to Xavier University which used to be our reg-ular biking and walking path past Potter Place and onto the Wonder Bread store located right at Dana Avenue and Woodburn. (Sometimes Mom would send us there, and we would come back with over a dozen loaves of bread... they would be eaten within a week in our house). Carl and I would ride even further north onto the campus of Xavier University (run by Jesuit priests, the college that Bobby attended) all the way through the campus to where it ended on Victory Parkway. We would even attend masses occasionally at Xavier's Bellarmine Chapel. Beautiful brick cottage houses surrounded the campus, and Carl had a paper route that covered them all up and down Woodburn and Dana. (Similar to how we passed jobs to each other through Skyline Chili, Fran and Chico first had the paper route here and showed him how to do so on his own). Carl (and all my brothers) learned their way around Evanston well at an early age on their bikes, so needless to say, they were all physically fit.

The construction project built a bridge across Montgomery Road (Aunt Chick's apartment building right at the end of that bridge at Jonathan Avenue), since this was a major thoroughfare through Cincinnati (it runs from Evanston to Montgomery, Ohio just north of the city). However, the bridge connecting Woodburn on our side of the neighborhood would not be completed until a year or so later. We all saw it as a disruption to our neighborhood flow, and it definitely made Carl's paper route harder. But then we realized that this construction could be quite the wonderland of adventure for my brother and I. We were ever-curious (especially Carl) about what went on at that site, observing it occasionally from a distance. He and I used to have so much fun playing in the dirt around our house, making mud pies, mud houses, etc. This was bound to involve a *huge mound* of dirt in which we could revel. This was a very exciting prospect for us both. But Carl would get entranced at how the huge backhoes and tractors were moving the earth in large quantities. At the time we were too young to realize that this was a major highway in the making.

I started kindergarten at Evanston School in the late 60s; the school was situated just a few blocks further north of Evanston near Norwood (the neighborhood Mom had warned us to steer clear of to avoid any racial clashes). At this time, Mom was working as the Lead Dietitian and Cook at St. Mark school, and it was Carl's task to go get me after half-day kindergarten and escort me daily (keeping me safe which he always did in life) to the cafeteria at St. Mark, where Mom would just be cleaning up from serving lunch to the students and staff of St. Mark School. Sometimes we would occasionally stop briefly on the bridge to admire all the big machinery, but then we would continue crossing the busy, breezy Montgomery Road bridge heading up toward St. Mark before the noon bells rang from the church's scenic bell tower (Carl's deadline to get me to Mom). One day, one big backhoe was moving dirt to Carl's fascination, and he froze in place gazing at the machine (he was often quite the daydreamer). I yelled at him, "Carl, we gotta go or we're gonna get in trouble with Mom!" Right then, the bells began to ring in the tower and I took off running toward the church and school, already familiar with the route from past trips. I was rushing and rushing to get there before the bells stopped ringing and did so just on time! Then, in my young mind I felt relieved like I had accomplished a great feat until Mom asked me, "Where is your brother Carl?" Then I realized that we were *both* in trouble... again! Carl got a whooping, had to stand in the corner, AND was grounded for a while after that incident. I remember Mom shouting at him afterwards stating "follow instructions!!" I got my share of tongue-lashings too for not convincing him to stay on task. We were to keep each other in check, per Mom's instructions. We really didn't get away with anything with our clever Mom, but we surely took to heart following her instructions after that scary incident. After that, she also kept an even closer eye on us now, knowing our mischievous nature and how we just got into stuff... *together.*

Carl and I did everything together, and everyone put us together as if we were twins. At St. Mark School, we were both crossing guards, and proudly wore our bright orange sash belt showing up to school early in order to help the other kids cross Dana and Montgomery Roads to get to the school and to leave to go home each day. We were also assigned to help students cross the street at the Dana exit from I-71. One day I was coming back from my duties as a crossing guard, walking solo back to the school passing cars parked in front of the school. I looked to the left noticing that each car was empty car until I began approaching a car with a man sitting inside which I thought was strange, while all the other cars were abandoned. As I passed his lap came into view, and I realized his stiff penis was exposed and he was holding it! Although I knew what it was (having been raised with four brothers), I had never seen it like so, and that startled me as a young girl. I immediately took off running to the school, and up to Sr. Claire Louise's room on the 2nd floor where we dropped off our crossing guard equipment before class. When I saw her, I ran to her in a huff and told her what I had seen... I could see the concern in her face when I told her and she repeated it back to me, questioning me if I was sure. Then we both went to the window overlooking the front of the school, and I pointed to the car. Sr. Clair told me to go to class, and then she raced to the office (probably to notify Sr. Rose Helene and thereafter the authorities). I never knew what happened after that, but all of the crossing guards were all warned thereafter that "if you see strange persons around the school report it immediately!" Carl took particular care to watch after me as a crossing guard when we were on duty after that incident.

Being an altar boy, Carl knew every nook and cranny of the church like the sacristy where the priests and altar boys prepare for each service. The chancel houses the altar, and there was also a long narrow hallway behind it that no one sees which allows the priests to go from the sacristy (far right front of the church) to the choir gallery (far left front of the church) without being seen. One day I came to meet up with Carl after his altar boy practice, searching him out as I often would. Always the curious two and since everyone else had left, in the quiet of the church he took me on a little tour into some areas of St. Mark that I had never seen. After walking me through that long narrow hallway behind the chancel, Carl asked "Nay! Have you ever seen the top of the bell tower?" I shook my head no, eyes widening at the thought of scaling that tower. He said, "I know how to get up there! Come on!" And of course, I followed my big brother to see what new sights we could see in our beloved St. Mark Church that we felt like we owned in that moment. He took me to what looked like a closet door on the second floor of the back of the church (same level as the massive church organ). That "closet" door that I had not recognized before led to a stairwell with an iron spiral staircase that led to the top of the bell tower, and Carl cut on the light upon entering the bottom of the stairs. Then he went to hit the switch for the stairwell light (a second switch), and it did not come on to provide light to go up the stairwell. I remember Carl reaching back and demanding "Hold my hand, it's gonna be dark at first, but hold my hand... we'll come into the light at the top." So, trustingly, I grabbed my big brother's hand as we carefully scaled that iron spiral staircase which felt like an eternity, but I felt secure just holding Carl's hand. And he was right; the light began to pour in as we approached the top, and for 10 minutes we sat at the top of that tower together in silence enjoying an amazingly scenic view of Cincinnati from that perch point. We saw lots of bird poop up there too, but that was not our focus at that precious moment. Our exploring did not end there. After we carefully came back down the spiral staircase from the bell tower feeling exhilarated from being up that high, we began to roam around the huge organ on the second floor and behind the balcony of the church, which I had only seen from a distance previously while down in the church. Carl and I went behind the structure and were chasing each other when someone shouted "Hey! You up there! Who is that?" Carl and I stood still and hid. It was Father Dennis Kinderman, our church pastor, mentor, and close family friend. Then he recognized Carl's hair and my pony tails and said "Carl and Naomi, get down here right now!" After a good lecture from him, we were sent home. In trouble *together* again!

Another interesting thing happened involving Carl and I right in front of our mother in front of our house, much to her horror. Carl often "rescued me" from things that occurred when I tried to be like him. We both often scaled our driveway wall to play obstacle course and climb up the patio above daring who could do so quicker. Like the time when I tried to follow him in climbing the cemented wall in our driveway, but as I was climbing it the dirt behind the wall began to loosen and separate, leaving the entire cement wall and turf to fall back onto the driveway while I was still hanging on. While keeping us in view from the front porch, Mom saw the whole thing, but was too slow and distant to be able to respond to assist in any way. However, right before a 6 x 6 cement wall came crashing down on top of me, I quickly jumped back and caught my footing away from slab of cement that was about to crush me. Instead of that occurring, it crashed on the ground and broke to pieces on the driveway right before me. I stood there in awe looking at the broken cement that could have ended my life, and then I looked up and Mom and Carl who were rushing toward me screaming "Naomi!!!" In this instance, I saved my own life as they both watched in horror! Like many previous "situations" I found myself in, I got a hug and then a lecture about what I was supposed to do. It was the kind of guidance that a young rambunctious girl like me needed to not only grow up wisely, but to stay safe. But I would continue to innocently challenge the rules of what I was and was not supposed to do around our house and in our community, but I must have had lots of angels watching over me even then.

Once Carl and I were around the corner from our house on corner of Jonathan and Woodburn Avenues, playing with Paula and Michael Washington, like we often did. They lived on the top floor of the two-family flat there, and they also attended St. Mark Catholic School with us. Their grandmother would occasionally send me to the store to buy her "snuff". She would call my Mom and ask if I could go to the store for her, and Mom would tell me to go to her house and get the money to go to the store. When I got to Blair Store (on Blair Avenue just a few blocks away straight up Woodburn) "Mr. Leon" would have it in a brown paper bag ready for me once I gave him the money for it. Any change, Grandma Washington would let me keep, and I thought that was such a gold mine that Carl and I always shared. Sometimes he would go with me, but she only asked for me when she called Mom. Once we lingered out in front their house on Woodburn playing with Paula and Michael (her grandchildren and our classmates at St. Mark). Along came Mrs. Richardson, a lady in the neighborhood that most knew took medication regularly and said strange things to the kids in the neighborhood, but she was always very nice and treated me to candies often. This day, she said she was "on her way to take the bus to get some ice cream", which sounded very interesting to me. Once I expressed interest, Carl looked at me sternly and said "Don't go, Nay... don't do it! You're gonna get in trouble!" But trusting that Carl knew who I was with, and Mrs. Richardson assured him "We'll be right back... it won't take long." So, I left with Mrs. Richardson, AND I was barefoot! Well, I later learned about why Mrs. Richardson needed to take medication. We went on a four-hour tour of Cincinnati, going from bus ride to bus ride, with no ice cream in sight, much to my disappointment. First, it felt like an exciting adventure going off on my own with Mrs. Richardson, but later I grew tired and hungry on the bus while traveling with her and realized the mistake I had made when it was too late. My mother must have been going bonkers hearing from Carl that her youngest child was traveling around Cincinnati barefoot with a woman who was on medication. The police eventually tracked down me and Mrs. Richardson after dark (I don't know how), but I remember getting a ride home in a police car. When I arrived, I got the same warm reception from my siblings as when I came home from the hospital, Carl looking at me angrily telling me "I told you NOT to go!" I knew then to pay attention to his warnings in the future. And Mom hugging me, feeding me a bowl of chili mac (the best I had ever tasted since I was ravenously hungry after hours away from home). But then I also got an ardent lecture from her about the importance of *never* "wandering off" on my own.

In my single digits I was still obsessed with following after Carl and just chasing him to see if I could have the same physical agility he did (we often chased one another to everyone in the house's dismay). I tried to mimic his every move. I remember my Mom, Mother Rob, Aunt Chick, Aunt Mabel, and every other adult tell us "Stop running in and out of this front door and use the handle!" Our front door (and screen door) would get a lot of traffic with so many in the house along with visitors. But in our haste, Carl and I ran through there often very quickly while playing, and in our haste, we would push the middle of the door (the screen section, or the glass if it got replaced for cooler months) instead of using the handle appropriately. Once Carl was chasing me, and again, as my Mom sat on the couch watching us running again (I think Aunt Mabel was there with her and her son, my cousin Darrell who was also our age and played close with us was probably close by too, part of the chase). Just as she shouted "Naomi, stop....!" I dashed forward escaping Carl (and Darrell too) and pushed on the, then, glass section of the door while running. Unaware that the handle to the door had recently been fixed by Mom, this time the glass gave way! The inertia I created from running forced my whole body to dive right through the glass section of the front door Superwoman style! But the glass ripped at my left arm as I went through, leaving it ripped open exposing much flesh and bleeding profusely. Seeing this horror on my own body, I began screaming my head off, something that sent everyone in my family running toward me. Mrs. Brown from directly next door must have heard the commotion, and after everyone in our house crowded me, she appeared with a first aid kit to initially wrap up my arm. Mom had Carl run across the street to the Warners to ask for a ride to the hospital, and Mr. Warner immediately came out and started up his car. He took us there and picked us up to bring us home afterwards. Weeks later after my scar had healed, Mom sat me down on the front porch, and Mrs. Brown (also a nurse) removed my stitches, and I was all good again. Thinking back, I was pretty brave to get the stitches removed with no anesthesia, but my clever Mom talked me through it as my siblings (and now Mrs. Brown's kids: Phyllis, Jerry "Lou", Norman, Jimmy also) observed Mrs. Betty Brown's awesome nursing skills at work. After that, I got a lecture from Mom about "you're growing into a young lady, and you shouldn't keep trying to do all those things that the boys do".

I took heed and eventually started gravitating toward my sisters (Cindy, in particular, who was happy to guide me and teach me about domestic things I should be helping with around the house, and how to care for myself physically as a maturing young woman. After I had my first period and started wearing bras, I stopped trying to follow Carl in *every* little thing he did (realizing he had a leg up on me being a tall, strong, growing young man). But from digging mud pies to bike riding to snow sledding to climbing around the house to watching TV together (like Jackson 5 cartoons on Saturday mornings or late-night scary movies with Bob Schreve's Past Prime Playhouse together), I loved tagging along with my big brother, my "twin", with whom I had so much fun throughout our childhood and of whom I treasure so many sweet memories. Out of all of my siblings, I must say that I am the closest in soul and spirit to Carl since we were hanging buddies and quite the duo as children.

As we got into high school, I began going to an all-girls school (Ursuline Academy) and he started theological studies (making considerations to possibly become a priest) at the all-boys Brunnerdale Seminary in Canton, Ohio. After being a faithful altar boy at St. Mark Church for years, this was per recommendation to Mom from the priests there. He was home on some breaks in between semesters, but we did not see much of each other when

I started high school. I began to hang out with my girls Monica Berry (neighbor directly across the street on Grantwood who was about Cindy's age) and my bestie for life Deneen Robinson (neighbor who lived on the same side of the street as us on Grantwood, but further down the street), because we were all obsessed with roller-skating. We would religiously go to skate at THE Royale Skating rink in Walnut Hills every weekend (sometimes doing the all-night skate, when I would "spend the night" over one of their houses in order to do so). It was a cool, healthy past-time, and occasionally when Carl was home from Brunnerdale, he would go skating with us and they would ask us "Are y'all twins?" since we favored each other so much. Carl had grown into a big tall strapping man by then, so when he skated, Monica would have us laughing saying "he looks like the letter 'L' skating".

After his studies, he and I lost some contact while I went off to college and while he did some college at Miami University of Ohio. He now has a son (Stefan), and continues to live and work in the culinary arts in Cincinnati, as he can make a mean souffle and a cheesecake better than any of the well-known German bakeries in Cincinnati. He still continues to be my guide, my muse, my wise counselor, and one who can speak to my soul and my spirit. I have a closeness with Carl like none I have with my other siblings since we spent so much time together while young (and got into so much together). We know everything about one another, almost our next move. Of all my siblings, he is truly my fellow kindred spirit. Carl was also affectionately called "Jug Head" by Uncle Bill, and we all mirrored this moniker for him just to be funny.

*****

All of my siblings mean the world to me, and they each have individually guided me to where I am today. Each of them, in their own way, are personable and courteous, capable and skilled, helpful and supportive, unintimidating and non-judgmental, strong and persevering, and all driven by family and faith (God). We all have bonded closely with one another over time as we grew up through our many hilarious, adventurous, tragic, and sometimes even dangerous experiences together over time. We are indeed one another's best friend. In any hour of need we encourage each other to reach out to one another for support, and it is never turned away. We check on one another, ensuring we're all doing well. If we don't hear from someone in a while, we're picking up the phone. And when we do talk on the phone to one another, we always laugh, confide, share, and can just talk with each other at length like really good friends do. I am so glad that God blessed me by having me be born into this family, even with all its challenges. But we all work any challenge through *together.* That has never changed. We were all taught to be this cohesive way in order to survive life as well as to live out God's plan for us. But we had no idea of the incredible situations and the storms that we were about to endure together that would bond us even tighter.... *forever.*

*"But as they sailed he fell asleep: and there came down a storm of wind on the lake; and they were filled with water, and were in jeopardy." – **Luke 8:23***

Chapter 5:
"Buddy" & "Sissy" - Our Loving, Faithful Parents

---

*"Honor thy father and thy mother that the days may be long upon the land which the Lord thy God giveth thee." – **Exodus 20: 12***

"Buddy" or Robert Lee Kinney, Sr. ran a strict household when he was home and not working. We lived in a neighborhood where there were lots of other big families, so kids ran amuck on our side street in our seemingly sequestered little black neighborhood of Evanston, where everyone cut their lawns regularly and the American flag was evident during all the summer holidays. Our house was particularly regimented, from what I remember and from what I hear in memory from my siblings, because of my father's strict ways. As the youngest of all nine, and according to my siblings, I did not receive the brunt of pain that my father inflicted during punishments that were issued regularly. My older siblings, particularly, my older brothers, received a lot of Daddy's lashings. There's the story of how one of my aunts sent her son (my cousin Juan) to our house so that Daddy could "straighten him up." Daddy tied Juan to a pole in our basement and beat him with a belt until he could not speak. Mother Rob had to go down there and stop him. It didn't do much good though; my cousin (and his brother) has been incarcerated often. I don't know if those whippings did any good, but they had a way of curtailing the wild activities of my cousins (and my brothers) then.

We all remember Daddy as a man that was meticulously clean and had to have everything neat, tidy, and in order. Mom said that all of his papers, checkbooks, and letters on his desk were kept in specific order, and she learned a lot from him. Ever-precious to him, had a way of cleaning his music albums that kept them scratch-free, and my brother Al ("Chico") told me that Daddy would not allow him or Fran to touch them to keep them that way. He would put the records in a certain order, and if he came back and they were out of order, they were in trouble. Chico also told me that Daddy used to come home and put on a record, and he and Mom would dance to the music. I remember those days. While they danced, Chico remembered that he would hold onto Daddy's legs and balance himself on his feet while both Daddy and Mom danced together (so that he could dance along with them as a threesome). It was a lot of fun he remembers. They told me that Mom and Daddy were into running a traditional home where the man was the bread-winner and the woman stayed home and took care of home. Mom would put on a clean apron and some lipstick before Daddy came home to be present-able for him. And she also made sure that the house was neat and clean and that dinner was ready (and/or had a cool glass of water ready for him if it was a hot day).

Daddy, born in 1929 into a large Catholic family typical of Cincinnati, grew up in a strict environment under his parents Sherman and Marie Kinney, and he spoke very properly like his older brother George. He grew up in a family of 15 children, and he was one of the middle children, all of whom lived through the Great Depression of the U.S. (1929-1939). My grandfather Sherman, Sr. died just before I was born, so I never knew him. Grandmother Marie Kinney was a very strict Irish woman, and she also lived in Evanston on Hackberry near (then) Purcell High School with my Aunt Marie (her cognitively challenged youngest daughter, who we called "Aunt Plukey" who was always a delight to me as the youngest, but not always so in the eyes of my older siblings). From what I hear, Grandmother Kinney and my father were not very close in their relation-ship; my grandparents just had so many children – he probably never got all the love that he wanted from them which happened a lot in large families. She didn't smile a lot, and when we visited she would gaze over us quite a bit (kind of inspecting us), probably amazed that her son had so many children like she did. We had to pray a lot, wash a lot, and had to be quiet a lot as children at her home. Grandmother Kinney often referred to us in her heavy Kentucky accent as "chirren" (Daddy was born in Covington, a small city right across the river from Cincinnati where everyone goes to get their liquor now since it is only sold in "state stores" in Cincinnati), and we would come running obediently. I remember she always had candy on display at her home during our brief visits, but we were *not* allowed to have any of that candy. I was thinking "What in the heck is the candy there for anyway?" in my little rational mind. I know my siblings felt the same too... seemed like torture. Although she was always very nice and courteous to us, I never quite felt the same warmth and grandmotherly comfort that came from "Mother Rob" (my mother's mother). She seemed distant yet obligated.

I could never tell whether or not Grandmother Kinney was white or black... she spoke so country, looked so fair-skinned, and had gray eyes that looked through those thick glasses that we would refer to as "Coke bottles." But she had long beautiful smooth, thick hair that cascaded down her back, but she always wore it in a "grandma" bun on the very top of her head. I only saw it down once (when she was fixing the bun in the mirror once), but I almost never got the chance to see it swinging freely... she would never allow that, so it was always in that bun. It always looked like a LOT of hair was up under that bun. I later asked Mom "Is Grandmother Kinney black or white?" Mom said "she's black, sweetie", but I still question that to this day, believing that she is surely of mixed heritage. I was told by one of my cousins on the Kinney side of the family that she was adopted, and that no one knows exactly who her parents were (nor are they exactly sure what her race is). I speculated that she might be one of those many children born to a Black-women, but sired by a white slave owner. It has always been a mystery to all of us.

We had attractive parents *(see photo insert)* who were admired by many for their handsome appearance as a young couple and their great love for one another. Both fair-skinned, they almost looked like siblings themselves, except in size. My mother "Freda" was a petite, small-built woman with Indian red skin and a broad, smooth nose that also screamed of her Native American roots from Gaffney, SC (Cherokee Indian). She had contrasting dark green eyes. She and her twin brother Alfred ("Uncle Sonny") were born in July of 1935 just as the Depression was ending, but for many Blacks in Cincinnati at the time living in the West End living conditions were deplorable and daily life was still very hard. "Sonny" and "Freda" both looked a lot alike in facial features, stature, and demeanor, but he did not have the same emerald green eyes that my Mom did and was slightly darker in complexion. Mom was a very attractive woman *(see photo insert),* but when I was young she was very modest and feminine in her appearance and dress. Mom and Daddy were a very loving couple, and treasured their growing family and their faith (the Robinsons were Baptist, but Mom converted to Catholicism when she married Daddy on June 30, 1952 (he was 22 and she was just 17 years old). My father was a tall, meaty man with very smooth, fair-skin, hazel grey-green eyes that looked like the crescents of the moon when he smiled. He had bushy eyebrows to go with those smiling eyes, and smooth dark curly hair that made him attractive to many of the women of his day. But he ONLY had eyes for Alfreda! After living through the Great Depression with all those Kinney siblings, Mom's beauty was a welcome sight for Daddy's sore eyes at the time. After they connected, they seemed inseparable. That's pretty obvious with the resulting nine children! As an adult, I was later told by a member of St. Mark Church (Mrs. Laura Banks who was also our school's secretary and worked closely with Sr. Rose Helene Wildehaus the principal and Father Dennis Kinderman the rector) about how my father would serenade my Mom outside their little apartment on Irving Street in the Avondale section of Cincinnati (before we got our house). She told me how everyone would talk about the sound of my Daddy's voice and how it would make all the other neighbors come outdoors also to enjoy hearing him serenade my Mom. "No wonder they ended up with so many children," our former church neighbor later told me and then smiled at me also saying "and *you* came from all that love!"

However, eventually Mom and Daddy on Grantwood would come into conflict at home over priorities with the kids or where Daddy had been for the evening. Sometimes when he would come in the door and sit at the kitchen table, coat still on, he would just ponder there for a moment. But Mom would come into the kitchen as soon as her husband arrived to attend to him, asking how he was doing or what he needed. She always made him a glass of water as soon as he arrived. He eventually saw this doting as irritating. "Don't watch over me, Sissy, I'm a grown man!"

"Well, I'm not watching over you, but I just want to talk to you and want to know if you're ok, Buddy. The kids have been asking a lot of questions that I can't answer. And they have a lot of needs. They need *both* of us, Buddy!"

"Don't remind me!"

Then he'd race out the door in a huff before my mother could say anything else. If he was not running with his pal (another Evanston neighbor) Joe Abraham, and another sly character from the West End named Tyrone Jacobs, he was running down the street to Brewster Street where the local recording studio called "King Records" was only two blocks away. Mom never really knew how much he was honing this talent for singing, because he thought that Mom would see it as a waste of time and not making money to support the family. But he visited King Records as often as he could to sing his heart out (probably to relieve a lot of the stress of raising a big family). He could also be among other budding creative artists at the time, and to get a release from the stress of the poverty that all Black families in Cincinnati (and in the U.S.) were experiencing at the time. For a while it also took him away from arguments with the wife that he loved very much, but felt some pressure from to be the best father and husband he could.

I later discovered that they also had other battles behind closed doors about Daddy's forgetfulness and lack of concentration. He would forget the simplest things, things that he was normally meticulous about before (such as shining his shoes regularly). At the dinner table, some of the kids

finished, but Carl and I (the two youngest) remained finishing our dinner with Mom and Daddy present.

One day, Mom said to Daddy: "Your buddy Joe Abraham
called today to say that he would be willing to help you
fix the hole that the kids made in the back porch. He just
needs to know a date and time, ok?" It got silent. Mom and
Carl looked at Daddy, and he did not move. He looked cata-
tonic for a moment. "Buddy! Buddy!" Mom shouted louder
and louder. Carl and Mom looked at each other very puzzled, me too young to realize what was happening. Daddy
eventually got up from the table in a huff, took his plate
into the kitchen, cleaned it off, and went to bed. He never
responded to my Mom and you could see the hurt and
confusion on her (and Carl's) face, although she tried to
act normal in front of us, telling us "Daddy is just tired."

I learned a lot about my father later in my life, like the
fact that he had this beautiful singing voice, but that he
also transitioned from working as an elevator operator to
working at the well-established Heeken Canning Company
on the West Side of Cincinnati with my Uncle Gus Robinson
(my mother's brother... his brother-in-law – Uncle Gus
helped him get the job). Initially, I was not sure which
branch of the military Daddy fought in, but Fran later told
me that he served in the Army during the Korean War and
that he wanted to be sent to Ireland (land of his Irish roots
as a Kinney). But Ireland "did not want any colored sol-
diers from the U.S. on their island". So, Daddy was sent to
remote locations like Greenland and Alaska instead. (I've

been to Anchorage and Valdez, Alaska, and found this to be an intriguing fact about my father... something that we have in common!). I remember seeing his green, wool service uniform folded and neatly boxed in our attic that Mom used to keep as a special treasure. I just remembered grabbing, smelling, and just holding it, treasuring the fact that my father wore that. My older cousins informed me that Daddy was good at "passing" (for white) when he kept his hat on; he could be accepted in some places. But when he took his cap off, he would get in trouble when they would see his wavy brown hair, as beautiful as it was. I remember running my fingers through it often when he would pick up me and my brother Carl (the youngest) and we'd be as high as his head. I would grip his head and hold his beautiful, soft locks of hair... I remember his hair, that handsome face, and those smiling crescent-shaped Irish eyes.

In his better moods, Daddy liked playing games with his many children as we grew up on Grantwood. We would get in to a match of "Hide and Seek," and Daddy would put my brother Carl and I either on top of the refrigerator (together) or each individually in the drawers of one of our dressers. He always promised to come back to get us after the "jig was up", and he always did come back and rescue us from our place there. Ceal and Chico remember Daddy piling us all into the pink station wagon to go to the Twin Drive-in on the weekends, a hallmark activity for Cincinnati families. We would all get in the car and go there and play in the playground area in front of the screen before the movie began. Then when they started playing anything risqué on the screen, Daddy would shout "Uh-oh, time for us to go!" I do remember that he kept that car parked *across* the street from our house all the time, right in front of the huge salt can for Grantwood. He probably did that to keep his car windows from being broken by (us) kids playing ball in the middle of the street, which was a common occurrence on Grantwood.

But Daddy soon became very troubled, and started doing other strange things besides just occasionally blanking out. My Mom noticed his forgetfulness, and my siblings noticed him staring into space and blanking out too. My brothers and sisters saw it (but it wasn't evident to us younger siblings like Cindy, Carl, and I... we were just too young). But my many older siblings began to notice how Daddy was changing. He was with us physically, but he was slowly "leaving us" mentally.

Chapter 6:
All About the Music

During the late fifties and early sixties in Cincinnati, R&B, country, and "rockabilly" (combination of rock `n roll and hillbilly music from Appalachia) were all popular forms of music. The mix of black and white culture occurring right at the Mason-Dixon Line (the Ohio River) made for an interesting mix of race, culture, and history in this region. I had no idea how my existence carries a taste of this... music is in my blood, part of my heritage, and now I know why. This love of music has often brought us together in Cincinnati (still does today), and I found out that a lot of good music came out of Cincinnati, and the Evanston community in particular. My father was one of those talents, I later found out. I'm sure that me and all my siblings got our intrinsic love of music from our father in particular.

As I was growing up, everyone told me that "all the 'red-bones' in Ohio (light-skinned black women in particular) come from 'the Nati'." I knew then that I had come from a special region of the state of Ohio where black and white confronted each other right on the Mason-Dixon line (sometimes on in a good way, but often negatively), but out of it unique to our region of Ohio resulted in a lot of children that looked like me (light-skinned Blacks). This was indeed a regional physical characteristic, and I would only realize it when I left Cincinnati to attend college, and someone would comment on my appearance. Cincinnati then and to this day struggles with the blend (or some say "clash") of the black and white cultures. Racial tensions in Cincinnati bothered and stressed everyone I knew who was Black, and when I got to college, I learned of the same patterns occurring with my classmates in other major cities from where they originated. My family (my father in particular) surely struggled with this as well on top of his family history and all his other personal challenges of managing a large family. It was compounded stress, and it challenged him and his sensitive nature daily, probably in an even more extreme way with what was occurring in our country during the 50s and 60s.

Daddy liked to sing, and he had a beautiful singing voice. Right there in Evanston was a spot where he (and many other well-known artists of the time) could showcase his talents. At 1540 Brewster Avenue in Evanston sat King Records, a recording studio started by Syd Nathan, a short, bald Jewish guy with unlikely connections to the black and country music circuit at the time, followed by the also well-connected Hal Neely. James Brown was one of the major recording artists who worked with Neely to record on wax at King Records where they were said to be playing "race records". *(James Brown then recorded with "The Famous Flames", and he later became "the Godfather of Soul".)* Nathan and Heely were in search of the local talent from around the Mid-west and Appalachian region to put their sound on wax. They also dropped in on the "talent nights" at the local high schools like Withrow High School (where Daddy attended) to see who was performing. Later they'd ask them to come to the King Records studio on Brewster in Evanston to record their voice and put them on wax. That's how Otis Williams and the Charms were discovered. A popular venue of the day in Evanston (now historic), King Records employed the likes of Little Esther, The Dominoes, Lula Reed, Charlie Gore, the Stanley Brothers, Joe Tex, Buck Owens, Johnny "Guitar" Watson, Hank Ballard & the Midnighters, Little Willie John, Freddie King, Edwyn Conley, Philip Paul, and later the popular "Cincinnati's Own" Bootsy Collins. Daddy was also one of those artists who was "tapped" at talent night at Withrow, and there were many other young wanna-be artists that frequented the recording studios of King Records, not only to listen in at other artists recording, but to do some of his/their own. Daddy had a beautiful voice, and he really only got a couple of chances to actually record there. I was too young to know that Daddy sang at King Records, but he surely would sing at home! *(My Aunt Mabel - his sister - told me about his singing at King records when I was an adult. Then my curiosity took off, and I've been trying to locate the actual recordings of my father - Robert Lee Kinney, Sr. - from King Records ever since.)*

The owner Syd Nathan had started in that building initially selling phonographs (record players) in the 1940s. Famous artists of the time like "Grandpa Jones" who played the banjo recorded his first hit at King Records in 1944 called "It's Raining Here This Morning". Grandpa Jones would go on to be famous on the country variety show with Roy Clark, Buck Owens, and Minnie Pearl called "Hee-Haw". He used to do the funny skit while looking through the window called "What's for Supper Grandpa?" where he would describe in true country and poetic fashion what's on the stove. But eventually Syd Nathan's shop would be the only place in the Midwest to record artists like Grandpa Jones, put him on wax (in that very building), package the record, and have it playing on the radio days later. There are stories that they would pile a bunch of 45s in a car after production and literally drive them to nearby radio stations pushing the hits, and sometimes as far as Tennessee or all the way up north to Detroit, Michigan in competing Motown territory. And in two to three days that song that was just recorded could be heard on the local radio, something very innovative at the time. With this innovation, King Records (and Syd Nathan) began to make a name for itself. My brothers Fran and Chico reminded me how, when they were young boys, they would steal the discarded broken 45s out of the dumpster behind King Records when they were young. They hung around outside the building and occasionally would hear some of the artists from the outside as they practiced what would soon be recorded. They would bring those warped 45s home and then tried to play them on our Hi-Fi stereo that Daddy forbade them to use.... but they tried anyway. I wonder if Daddy's voice was on any of those tossed 45s(?). In 1963, the year I was born, a plane crash killed the famous Patsy Cline, but also on that plane was "Cowboy Copas" who was another artist who recorded at King records. When I turned three my father started taking great interest in visiting King Records.

At that time, Henry Glover was one of the studio executives that reported directly to Syd Nathan. This "race music" (music by African-American artists) was becoming more and more popular at "Queen Records" named after Cincinnati being the "Queen City", now the R&B portion of King Records. Inside is where there was a production company, a studio, and a business office. The name "Race music" originally came from a history of church recordings (sermons and sometimes religious skits) that began to play on the radio in the 1920s. Early recordings of Rev. Clarence LaVaughn Franklin known as "C.L." from Detroit (Aretha Franklin's dad) could be heard on the radio talking about how "The Eagle Stirreth Her Nest" or the other preachers on the radio displayed their "Mississippi Hoop" preaching style where they sang the sermon. This gravitated many in the Black community to listen to the radio more, a popular pastime in this era.

However, decades later at stations like King Records, songs with enduring themes containing rather risqué subject matter for the time began to be heard on the radio, and became even more enticing for those interested to hear.

Songs recorded on the Queen/King label were songs like "I Guess I Better Get Up and Go Home" by Rusty Diamond, and "Crazy Vietnam War" by David "String Bean" Akeman. Syd Nathan and Henry Glover aggressively sought out talented local artists like Daddy at the time, trying to get them to come to the Brewster Avenue recording studios to put their sound on wax. He and Syd not only sought singing talent, but they also wanted song-writers too. He was a good friend and one who would give Daddy constructive and honest feedback. From what I've learned my father talked with Henry often about his family situation. He never told Glover, however, about the feeling of being overwhelmed and that he often heard voices. My father was very troubled at the time, and his singing and music were his only outlets in his mind at the time that allowed him to express himself (expressing himself was something a black man in the 60s in any US city, namely Cincinnati, Ohio, was NOT encouraged to do).

Besides just stopping through during the week, Daddy came to the studio early each Saturday morning specifically to meet up with Henry and other "studio rats" who would coach him and give him some special attention before the bigger, more well-known acts came through to do their business in the studio. Reggie gave special attention to Daddy since they went to Withrow High School together. Henry had a growing concern about what he was hearing in the neighborhood and from others at the studio, and what he was personally observing about my father's changing behavior and mood. Daddy recorded two songs that did not do well on the regional promotions circuit: "Eternal Love" and "Come with Me Tonight".* The lack of success of his recordings added to the anxiety levels that "Buddy" Kinney experienced month after month of going to the studio each weekend, after working his 9-to-5 job at Heekin Canning during the week. It was 1966, a tough time in Evanston and Avondale and all Black communities across Cincinnati (and in many major cities), but King Records was going full swing with close to 300 employees (both black and white together) working at the shop at 1540 Brewster in Evanston. At the same time, Daddy had two songs that were not successful and the pressure of a house filled with a wife and nine children, all needing to be fed. He felt trapped. But Daddy apparently still walked the two blocks down to Brewster as often as he could in order to feed his talent (and to free his mind).

What a history lesson I learned that connected Cincinnati history with the history of my father through King Records, one of the many historic aspects of southwest Ohio! As an adult, I was really intrigued and had to do a little more digging to find out more about him and his life that I apparently missed being so young when he died. Boy, did I find out some interesting things about not only him, but also about Evanston, and the history of King Records!

During its 30-year history, King Records has had over 30 Rock and Roll Hall of Fame Inductees record there. Those previously mentioned include other artists like, Dave Bartholomew, The Royales, Professor Longhair, Les

Paul, and Otis Williams. King Records eventually closed its doors in 1968 when Syd Nathan died, and has been used as a storage facility since 1973. A marker has been placed on Brewster Avenue to commemorate the history of King Records in the Evanston neighborhood, something that many Cincinnatians don't even know about. When I returned to Cincinnati in 2005, I found out about this and searched for the historic placard that now appears in front of the warehouse where they made and shipped 45s in the late 50s and early 60s. Only by accident, when I was driving down Interstate Highway 71 did I see the placard! I then realized just how close King Records was to 1607 Grantwood. In October of 2019 the City Council of Cincinnati voted to form the King Records Legacy Committee, and they are trying to revive the historic place in Evanston that was known as the "birthplace of rock and roll".

(Refer to previous map of Evanston to see how close King Records on Brewster Avenue was to 1607 Grantwood Avenue in Cincinnati, Ohio where I grew up. *My father's song titles and King Record executives' names are fictitious, but all other information about King Records is factual.)

* * * * *

The months rolled by and times grew harder in all the Black communities across Cincinnati like the West End, Price Hill, Avondale, and Evanston in the late 1960s. It was a time of great unrest, the Civil Rights Era, and blacks were limited as to where they could go in the predominantly white Cincinnati. There was rampant systematic racism in housing, education, and in job opportunities. Then there was the neighboring community of Norwood that was notorious for its anti-black sentiments, who let us know to our face that we (as Blacks) were not welcome to cross over those railroad tracks and into their community just blocks from my grade school and from King Records. As she sat in her rocking chair in the dining room right up under her cuckoo clock that would sound on the hour, I would hear my mother (Alfreda) advising my older siblings before they would head out the front door: "no, you can't go over there" (Norwood) or "you shouldn't be seen down there" or to several other places they wanted to go. And then she would tell them "it's just not safe for Black people there now." I didn't understand so much about all that until an occasion when I was walking through Norwood with my brothers and sisters. We went to a popular shopping center there (located just at the end of Evanston and the beginning of Norwood) called Twin Fair. Once on the way back from Twin Fair with my siblings, three white kids (boys) passed us on the sidewalk. When we walked past them, they turned around and started hurling pop bottles at us from afar. One of the pop bottles came very close to grazing my head, and it infuriated my brother "Chico" (Alfred). Mom never let us go into Norwood without at least two of my big brothers with us. Chico wanted to fight them, but my other brother Francis who was also with us told him "don't do it!... they've got a lot more support here than we do." So, we had to quickly retreat to Evanston angry, but without injury or confrontation. We talked about that for days among us, about what had just happened from which we could not defend ourselves and questioned why. I learned that day that the world outside of our idyllic neighborhood was a tough one, and that I had to prepare myself for some tough times coming up, especially if I was to be on my own away from the protection of my siblings eventually. I (we) had no idea how tough the world really was/is...

Daddy while working each week at the Heekin Canning Company in downtown Cincinnati also tried to make his music career blossom at King Records (or he hoped to be on the local WLW Radio that often featured many local artists, but most were white). But it was hard for Black acts to get an opportunity to be selected to be on that station (being fair-skinned like Daddy still brought no better advantage than any other Black when it came to jobs and employment). And when he worked within the Black community, he still got called "high yellow" by some of his peers who envied his handsome appearance. It was hard to tell whether he was black or white (just like his mom, Grandmother Marie Kinney). So, a lot of other people couldn't decide either, and this probably made it hard for him to fit in anywhere. I'm sure this generated a lot of anxiety for him where he did not feel very well-supported. On one hand, he was never white enough, and on the other hand, he was never black enough.

His handsome appearance that normally should attract others (and often it did, like my Mom), it eventually proved to be very frustrating for him. He was criticized for his color by some of his black "friends", but was also devalued and dehumanized on a daily basis by the white community just like any other black man during this time. Even with Reggie's occasional coaching at the studio and with my Mom's immediate support and understanding at home, his position in life brought him some grief on a daily basis. The men, heads of households, in the black community at this time often became emasculated, and each dealt with these societal pressures in their own unique ways, family to family: some physically left their family scene altogether never to be seen again (leaving many fatherless children in the black community). Some stayed and reverted to drinking or drugs, some took it out on their spouses (and sometimes the children too) in the form of domestic violence, and some just checked out mentally – each a heavy burden for their families left behind in the aftermath. My father began to do the latter (mentally check out), I believe from a combination of societal pressures and his own psyche telling him he was inadequate (but at this point I can still only guess at how much pain he was in). Even with Daddy's unique singing skills and beautiful well-admired family, Buddy still found it hard to be "successful" in his own mind, and this proved to be very frustrating for him and our family when I was a very young girl. And now I know why there was no tenth child.

Ironically, the devaluation of Black lives continues in cities all across America to this day, and this has to stop. When an act of prejudice occurs against anyone, it not only harshly affects that individual person's psyche and their belief in themselves, but it affects their entire family and community around them. Prejudice is ugly and so are its after effects: frustration, hate, division, violence, crime – all directed toward one another and sometimes toward ourselves. We have seen this throughout U.S. history occurring repeatedly across all our communities nationwide, but we continue to stay so divided, knowing the harsh effects of our division. Hate is still being taught across generations, and we are moving further and further away from God. So much about our country has changed, but so much is still the same. We all need to know that LOVE instead is the answer, ending our destructive behavior toward one another, and that being "Christ-like" to one another is more ideal and productive for all our communities.

Kids of King Pictures

Robert Lee, Sr. & Alfreda Robinson Kinney

Alfreda Robinson Kinney & Robert Lee Kinney, Sr.

Robert Lee Kinney, Sr. (dark jacket) behind Grandmother
Kinney (and his siblings, the other Kinney children who are
my aunts and uncles)

Life in the West Side of Cincinnati from 1940s
(front: Uncle Arliss and Alfreda Robinson – mom;
back row (unknown lady and Aunt Helen)

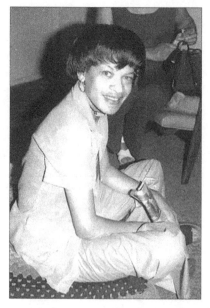

Alfreda Robinson Kinney (seated)

Angela (sister), Mom, and Jonathan (nephew, Karen's son)

Naomi at 10 years old (tomboy)

Naomi with Uncle George, Aunt Kathleen, and Jennifer (niece,
Karen's daughter – picture taken by Uncle Billy Connell,
husband to my Aunt Ethel who was sister to my
father and George)

The Kinney Sisters: Karen, Cecilia, Cynthia, Angela, and Naomi

Kinney siblings at Carl's wedding. From left to right
(in order of birth): Bobby, Karen, Chico, Fran, Angela,
Cecilia, Cynthia, Carl, and Naomi.

Kinney siblings at St. Mark Family Reunion, last time in the cafeteria. From left to right *(in order of birth):* Bobby, Karen, Chico, Fran, Angela, Cecilia, Cynthia, Carl, and Naomi.

Namesake Naomi Frazier and my daughter Julia

Naomi at college graduation from
Central State University (OH)

Naomi at work
(with Delta soror Ingrid Williams)

Aunt Mary Robinson (with daughters Kim, Carol, Diane and
family friend) and Kinney girls (Karen, Angela, and Naomi)

Carl and Naomi (at family reunion in Gaffney, S.C. in 1991)

Chapter 7:

This Too Shall Pass

*"Let destruction come upon him at unawares; and let his net that he hath hid catch himself: into that very destruction let him fall." – **Psalms 35:8***

Jonathan Park was located on Jonathan Avenue... three blocks from our home on Grantwood in Evanston. It was the place that we all would go to get out of the house (and away from our big families) to swing on the swings, climb on the monkey bars, play tether ball, or bounce around on the spring-loaded horse rides cemented into the ground there. If you stand in the middle of the street on Jonathan and look east you can see the beautiful structure of St. Mark Church three blocks ahead of you sitting on perpendicular Montgomery Road, the church that many of us in our close-knit black middle-class community attended. We would also ride our bikes through the open area in the park, which leads to tennis courts belonging to nearby Walnut Hills High School and onto the property of the historic Lane Seminary, sometimes doing so barefooted. The high school campus began on the back edge of the park and was clearly in view. Between the park and the tennis courts was a parking lot where the park patrons could park. It was also a tailgaters paradise. A lot of parties went on there (often in the cars) in that parking lot. My Daddy and his neighborhood chums found themselves there partying one cold, confusing afternoon in the winter of 1966.

As "Buddy" began to drink more and more while sitting in the driver's seat, he fell more and more into a depressive state as his buddies rattled on about the events of their day. *(I later found out that more and more he got into these depressive states and had to leave our house on Grantwood to "get his mind right" before returning home to his full house. My mother had rescued him before from this depressive state that were slowly gaining in frequency, twice previously having to pull him from a running car in our closed garage.)* This time Daddy had purchased a gun from his West End buddy Tyrone. But Tyrone at the time had no idea how he had planned to use it, nor did he question Daddy about it during the purchase. This particular afternoon, Daddy was upset, depressed, drinking, and silently toting that gun while sitting in that car with his two drinking buddies. Before they could even see what was happening, he pulled out a small black 38, and they saw him start waving the gun as he ranted on about all his problems during their conversation. They both froze not sure what his next move would be, but hoping it would not be what they thought. Before they could convince him to put it down, they heard the gun go "pop"... during his rant of frustration and anguish, Buddy put the 38 to his left temple and pulled the trigger, ending his life on the spot.

There were two neighborhood kids that discovered Daddy's in this state: Judson Ward and Alex "Buddy" Jackson. Alex's little brother "Mitchie" played and rode bikes with Carl often; they were the same age. Alex and Mitchie's dad and my father were very close; they had a big family like we did. Judson and Alex were two kids in the Evanston neighborhood that got into trouble often, and were just roaming up and down Jonathan Avenue on which the both lived (but closer toward the end near St. Mark). The also both attended St. Mark School and Church also. As the two youths approached the car, Alex said "Hey, ain't that Mr. Kinney's car?" Judson responded saying "Yeah! Let's go see what he's up to." As they both approached the vehicle, Judson arriving first and recognizing what had happened, Judson turned around quickly, blocking Alex's view of what was inside the vehicle: Daddy was alone in the vehicle and was slumped over the steering wheel. "Go home and tell your dad to come down here RIGHT NOW!", demanded Judson to Alex. Alex knew something was terribly wrong, and turned to run down Jonathan Avenue to his house to get his father. When he arrived, he ran into the house and shouted at his dad sitting in the living room "Dad, you gotta come to Jonathan Park NOW! Mr. Kinney is there in his car, and he's not moving!" Mr. Jackson, fearing the worst had occurred (and knowing Daddy's troubling demeanor lately), he ran around the corner to get Mr. Robinson another neighbor and friend who also lived on

Grantwood (our street). They both ran to Jonathan Park at top speed, passing (but not stopping at) our house to get there. When they arrived, they saw Judson there crying. Then Mr. Jackson, his good friend, broke out crying. By the time Alex, ever-curious, arrived back at the park on his bike, he saw his dad in the distance standing next to the car with his face in his hands sobbing openly. They had already called the police by then, and they were pulling up on the scene.

While on his bike running his regular paper route, my brother Chico (young Alfred) was the first to hear from the crowd about what had just occurred, and went running toward the park as crowds of neighbors began to gather. Then he ran into my sister Karen who told him "Don't go down there, Chico! Do NOT go down there, whatever you do!" She had to drag Chico back to our house, just a block away to keep him from going to see his dead father in that tragic state, an image that could have affected him greatly and change his young psyche forever. From what my siblings tell me (I was only three at the time), it was a horrible and shocking day for everyone in the entire community, especially my mother (Alfreda). Some said that she could not speak at all. Once she got this shocking news, how was she supposed to react in front of her children? What decisions did she have to make immediately regarding the care of her husband's body? How could she go on? I did not see Mom a lot after that, and she stayed in her room with only short visits from close family, friends, and neighbors trying to console her (and they always brought some food or gifts for the children when they did visit). It was a very tragic day in the community of Evanston.

We all needed at least 48 hours to get a grip and try to comprehend what had just occurred and to try to begin answering all the questions we were scared to ask. In one selfish moment, my father had taken his own life, not caring about the impact to those left behind. Or maybe he just could not possibly tolerate caring for us or considering us in his mental state at the time.

I later found out that my father had been officially diagnosed with **schizophrenia** at the time which is a chronic, severe, and disabling brain disorder. Schizophrenia is considered a long-term mental disorder that involves the breakdown of the relational thoughts between emotion and behavior leading to faulty perceptions of reality. He had been hearing voices that others didn't hear, and had been speaking in strange ways to my mother... she knew it, but probably tried to shield us from this as long as she could. People with schizophrenia get into states of withdrawal from personal relationships and into fantasy or delusion with much mental fragmentation. These individuals will often sit for long periods of time without moving or saying anything. On a few occasions at the kitchen table this would occur with Daddy, a place which used to be for loving, informative, loquacious exchanges between them, had become deafeningly quiet. Many people with this brain disorder have difficulty holding a job or caring for themselves, and they end up heavily relying on others for help in their most basic of daily tasks. It is a mental disease that is well treated today with new and innovative treatment options, but there were *no* options for my father in the late 60s (short of a few pacifying counseling visits to Longview Hospital, which has a long history of persons of Irish descent being sent there for a variety of prejudices typical of that community, and the name "Kinney" on their books for Daddy probably told them to treat him just as badly. This was a society and social climate in Cincinnati (and in America) where Black men, who are already hated just for being Black, surely would not have their plight understood nor would anyone want to treat or touch those Blacks who suffered from mental illness.

So, Daddy and Mom probably struggled greatly during the time of his mental illness well before his suicide, but Mom *also* had to continue to care for nine young children as well. Now, that I think back on this, she probably had to save face and be brave often in front of her children with what their father was going through while caring for each of our daily needs…. An amazing feat. I have even more respect for her now after exploring all these events of our tragic past.

"But doing this only two weeks before Christmas in 1966 seems cruel, Daddy", I say to myself decades later thinking of what had occurred on that fateful day in Jonathan Park's parking lot. "Buddy" decided to take his own life and leave his wife ("Freda") with nine children between the ages of three to thirteen to finish living our lives out in this aftermath. When I think back on what a crisis this must have been at the time, an immense sadness overcomes me even to this day. What a daunting task my dear Mom had to endure to wade through all of this. From what I heard, she was numb for many days afterwards, probably just in shock. I was too young to experience what my siblings did then, but I know that we all still ache from the result of his actions. (we) still do and always will definitely experience this event in our minds retroactively for the rest of my (our) lives.

The news of my father's suicide hit the entire Evanston community immediately like a ton of bricks, as people were literally running from door to door telling their neighbors of what they heard had occurred recently in nearby Jonathan Park. Where normally children run and play freely in the park, that day all of the children were told that they could not even play outside on that day, and they definitely were not allowed to go to Jonathan Park for weeks after that tragic event had occurred there. Additionally, news got back to those at nearby King Records also. Reggie and all who knew my Daddy at King Records were crushed, and production paused for a few days, everyone so disappointed at this tragic event and at such a great talent lost. They could not believe that my father had resorted to such measures and they felt bad that they never knew that he was in such mental turmoil, having possessed such a talented voice. They saw it as a loss to the local music scene there in Evanston. Many from King Records and from the local community who heard about the tragedy attended his service.

His younger children, unfortunately were not allowed to attend his funeral, and were taken to Mrs. Lattimore's home (who lived directly behind us on Clarewood). My older siblings, however, were indeed able to attend, and they have very sad memories of crying at Daddy's funeral with many of his siblings also present. The casket was closed anyway, considering how Daddy died, but I still don't know why they denied for all of us to attend at that time. This probably would have created a worse memory of my father for me and for my other siblings who didn't attend anyway. Nonetheless, since it was just before Christmas, from what I'm told, there was such an incredible outpouring of gifts and toys for all of us it would suffice for two Christmases for nine children! And ever since then, we received a LOT of community support from everyone in Evanston knowing that my mother would now be the sole provider for nine children after this tragedy. We received regular Thanksgiving and Easter baskets from the church (St. Mark) and baskets of food, gifts, housewares, appliances, and toys from many other community sources, family, and friends. And me and my siblings at that point, were insistent to make this thing work and support my mother within our now fatherless household in any way that we possibly could moving forward... *together*. News got around that the Kinney family had experienced the tragic suicidal death of their father Robert Lee Kinney, Sr. aka "Buddy" on December 19, 1966.

It was a hard time for blacks in Evanston; racial tensions in Cincinnati mirrored those riots and protests occurring in major cities across the United States. But Cincinnati in particular has a long history of race riots (along with many cities/states along the Ohio river). It is a history of wanting to keep Blacks out since the Emancipation Proclamation that freed slaves went into effect in January of 1863. There have been many white abolitionists (those who wanted to abolish slavery) that would assist Blacks to migrate from the south through Cincinnati by way of the "Underground Railroad", not actual train cars but instead a network of compassionate property owners (black and white) who would hide freed or runaway slaves on their premises until they made it far enough north to freedom. But they had to get through the harsh social disorder of "Jim Crow" laws and vigilante organizations (like the Klu Klux Klan) who terrorized, tortured, and killed those who would not follow these rules. They did not allow Blacks to move about freely, even though they were considered "free". Lynchings (hangings) increased in the 1890s throughout the U.S. (particularly in the South and Central U.S.), while many northern states like Delaware, Maryland, and Missouri supported the abolitionists.

However, Ohio and neighboring Indiana were not in support of the abolishment of slavery, and so permitted the vigilante groups to run amok and do as they please to many in these Black communities. Wherever there was a success of Blacks in their community, there was a group of white vigilantes ready to destroy it. So, the riots in Cincinnati began (and they continue) whenever people feel that their voices are not being heard. For Cincinnati, their long history of riots stem from the corrupt community environment of "living on the river" in the late 1800s along with the mix of immigrants trying to prosper there while Blacks were just getting their freedom, all in "the pursuit of happiness" and all seeking to establish the American Dream for their families. However, some thought (and think) that these basic liberties are more deserving of some of us than others. For whatever the reason, the history of destructive race riots in Cincinnati includes:

(Some facts taken from Cincinnati.com, from the Cincinnati Herald newspaper, and from Wikipedia)

- **1829** – Irish immigrants rioted homes of freed Black slaves for fear of job competition; they forced over 1000 Black families out of town (more than half the Black population at the time)

- **1836** – James G. Birney (an abolitionist and publisher from New York) owned a printing press that was burned down twice, because he started the Ohio Anti-Slavery Society and published newspapers targeting slaveowners in Ohio and Kentucky. During the April riots many Black homes were destroyed along with his printing press.

- **1841** – An angry mob of white German and Irish immigrants marched down Fifth Street in Cincinnati, and the group was armed with a cannon. They fired it down the street into what they called "Buck Town" (Black neighborhood along the river), and many lives were lost because of this action taken by the mob.

- **1884 – Cincinnati Courthouse Riots** was considered the most bloody in Cincinnati history, and was triggered by public outcry from a manslaughter verdict on a murder case over which many were in conflict. This was not really prompted by race, but over 50 people died in the riot and the Cincinnati Courthouse and the jail was burned to the ground and destroyed.

- **1935** – This riot quickly escalated from a fight between two students (one black and one white) who attended Oyler School in Price Hill. Police forced the closure of the Eighth Street viaduct to avoid the clash of groups of angry blacks and whites.

- **1967 – Avondale Riots of 1967** broke out over the festering and deplorable living conditions and police abuse that Blacks withstood during this time. Some of this was also prompted by the conviction of Posteal Laskey in December of 1966 of the murders of seven women in Cincinnati (the "Cincinnati Strangler"), but many in the Black community felt that the testimonies and evidence against him were circumstantial. Ohio National Guard was called to restore order, and President Lyndon Johnson's Commission on Civil Disorder stated that the riots were due to "the poverty of the segregated neighborhoods in Cincinnati and the practice of police officers in 'stopping Negroes on foot or in cars without obvious basis' and using loitering laws disproportionately against minorities".

- **1968 – Avondale Riot of 1968** was triggered by the death of Rev. Dr. Martin Luther King, Jr. when Blacks were terribly angry that their civil rights leader (and promise of a better future in America) was assassinated. After his death was announced, for two days looting, property destruction, and rioting occurred across Cincinnati, much by angry Blacks who were at their wit's end.

(1992 – Los Angeles rioted over the brutal beating of handcuffed, arrested Rodney King that was caught on videotape.)

- **2001 –** In April, Cincinnati police officer Stephen Roach shot and killed Timothy Thomas which sparked riots in the Over-the-Rhine neighborhood of Cincinnati. Charlie Luken (mayor of Cincinnati at the time) had to call in the National Guard to stop all looting, violence, and vandalization, mostly to police in the downtown area. This and a downpour of rain forced the three days of rioting to subside.

- **2020 –** Major cities across the U.S. erupted in protest over the death of George Floyd who was killed by Minneapolis, MD police officer Derek Chauvin by placing his knee on Floyd's neck for nine minutes, also caught on videotape for the world to see. Cincinnati experienced riots during this time in the Over-the-Rhine area of the city where many store fronts had their glass broken or were vandalized. Police in riot gear attempted to disperse a diverse crowd of people (not just Blacks protested) that had formed in Washington Park on the west side. Cincinnati police had to use helicopters and other tactics until 3am to get the riots to subside, but there was still much civil unrest across the city, especially in the Black neighborhoods.

This division between the black and white communities Cincinnati has continued for decades, much due to the systematic racism, oppression, and devaluation they have felt over time by the white community. It has always been a pressure-cooker of racial sentiments waiting to explode (some of this occurring in 2020 with the burst of the "Black Lives Matter" movement). *(And ironically, my father took his life in Evanston in 1966, physically situated right next to the Avondale community where we first lived, just before so much rioting erupted in Cincinnati in 1967 and 1968 – a clear demonstration of the stressful times for all Blacks in Cincinnati at this time.)*

Chapter 8:

The Stigma of Suicide Death

*Let us not therefore judge one another anymore:
but judge this rather, that no man put a stumblingblock
or an occasion to fall in his brother's way.*
– Romans 14:13

his was a particularly painful day in the idyllic Evanston community and for this normally admired big family. Where everyone used to complement our family on how "perfect" our family was, after my father's suicide many looked at us differently now. I wondered what other families in our community were dealing with the same issues of mental illness and suicide, or were we just the only unique family to be going through this?

It started as a lot of pity that the entire neighborhood felt for our family, then it progressed to a strange stigma we held as "those kids". I didn't even really realize that Daddy was not around until I was about 5, and one of my siblings (not sure which) had to break the news to me about "why Daddy wasn't going to be coming home anymore". It was a sad, hard reality to accept that our fun, loving, disciplining dad was gone *forever*. And I never got the chance to say "Goodbye, Daddy!" I felt angry in that moment of hearing that news. I just remember Mom being distant from me for quite a while when I was little, my older siblings directly caring for me instead of her. (This is something I definitely noticed, but did not think she didn't love me... I just knew she had a lot to handle with all of us and running our house. I thought my siblings were just helping her out in that regard.) We received lots of genuine, positive empathy for the tragedy that had occurred, but we also got "the look" wherever we went in the neighborhood... for years. And they would also awkwardly refer to "the thing that happened to your father" during different conversations (instead of openly talking about the suicide). But I now realize (as an adult) that we didn't really know how to respond to some of the comments and questions that we received then. It was and still is very hard to discuss openly without trying to answer all the questions (which we just couldn't, not knowing ourselves why it had occurred). You don't really know what to say sometimes *still*. But we all clung tight to one another, forming an even closer bond among us siblings in our plight.

My siblings and I had moved on in life without Daddy's physical presence, but he/his name would occasionally come up for personal business or during normal conversations about families, and we'd all have to handle a way to explain the situation and to explain away our hurt for what had occurred, as if it has not affected us. But the pain never really goes away. Shortly after my father's death, we did not see a lot of the Kinneys - only one of his siblings (Aunt Mable) did we see often. I rarely saw Grandmother Kinney for a while there also. When I did not see them, I started feeling like and realizing that my father's siblings, at some point, might have thought that we (his nine children) were to blame for his death. Maybe we caused his pressures and the anguish he had. It had to have been hard to have brought nine children into the world, discipline, and try to feed them in this difficult day and time in Cincinnati history. I now realize that these issues made it hard for him to be able to care for his children the way he knew they deserved. So, imagine having to later raise all of them *solo*, like my mother did! She managed to endure the pressure, so "why couldn't you, Daddy?" I would ask myself often. I want to blame him personally for "punking out", but I also want to blame some of the conditions of the time for people like him.... Not sure if either sentiment is validating of the situation for me. These and many other questions I've asked over the years. "Why?" is always a question of those who survive suicide I later learned, and after a while to end my own anguish, I stopped asking it. He must have had some reasoning in his mind or he must have been in such pain and mental turmoil. It's a done deal and sadly I/we (like many other survivors of suicide) must reticently accept it and try to move on in life, now allowing it to stifle or grip you too much (learning any lessons I/we can along the way).

Then there are those thoughts that everyone has about *you,* watching to see if you will do the same thing that your father did: commit suicide. There is the "Kinney Crazies" stigma that was placed on us all, insinuating that we are now just like our father. Well, I would *never* want to go that route. My faith is too strong and there are too many positive reasons to live. But most of all, I do NOT want my family or my child feeling about me the way that I felt/ feel about Daddy: angry, disappointed, hurt, and let down. Even if he was not perfect (and no one is) I felt like he should have just kept on being the great dad for us that he was (but he evidently just could not). I also hurt for my dear mother. I am also angry at him about how he left her without regard to how she could possibly handle things emotionally and how she would continue to raise their *nine* children alone financially and morally without a father... or maybe he just could not focus on that with his mental illness. Being the youngest, I still am always giving him the benefit of the doubt, guessing on his reasoning. But, according to my older siblings, this was not Daddy's first suicide attempt. Mom apparently had to rescue Daddy often after he made several suicide attempts! He put himself in our garage a few times with the car going and the doors closed... her little self pulled that big man out of there each time. He took a few overdoses of pills, and she called the ambulance to take Daddy to the place "with the white coats" where he would be "locked away for a while." This was puzzling terminology to us then, but we understand it all now. He was then diagnosed as "schizophrenic" (something I didn't learn about until I got into adulthood and was not talked about generally among families – I'm glad that's changing now). I'm glad that now it's ok to say "I'm *not* OK!"

To this day, when I tell people about my father's suicide it is shocking to them and I sometimes get that "look" again, their awkward response... many don't know what to say or how to react. And sometimes I don't want to shock people about my past, so I intentionally don't mention it at all or I have to find just the right time to mention that fact about my history to new friends I meet who may ask the question. If they bring it up first that it occurred in their family, then I'll add what happened to me, often as consolation for their loss. It was more of an issue when I was younger in grade school and high school when I would get the question "Where is *your* dad?" Now, I'm better equipped to handle the response or reaction that people have to the devastating loss that me and my siblings have had to endure for years. Again, I am ever-clear to let everyone know that I do NOT see suicide as a viable option in life... *ever.* God should be the only One deciding when a life ends/begins.... Not me. I can't even fathom the depth of pain in life that my father went through or the "dark moment" that he was in to get to that point, and I also could not even empathize with him until I started learning more about and trying to understand the root cause of his troubles: mental illness and schizophrenia.

In my twenties and thirties, I used to be ashamed of talking about depression and mental illness, and I definitely didn't want to talk about suicide, considering the stigma that comes with these things, and ironically one that could prompt another. I am pleased that now people are encouraged to speak up, notice the signs/symptoms of, and to report episodes of mental illness occurring within their families, friends, and acquaintances. Additionally, SO many more resources are available now for those suffering from mental illness; there are even mental health resources popping up in the small in-store grocery and pharmacy clinics where people are encouraged to stop in and speak to a counselor on demand. This world is too mean and crazy for us NOT to have these kinds of resources in place, especially for children who are impacted by those suffering from mental illness (or when they experience it themselves – it comes in many forms). Sometimes the family members around them need more counseling and support than the person who has been diagnosed!

My father's suicide was hard on us all then and I know that it has affected our view on the world. It was an extremely hard time on all of us, but it further strengthened the bond we already had, and forced us to commit to one another in a way that some families never experience. After learning so many life lessons, suicide survivors like us "Kids of King" (with a more faithful perspective focus on positive outcomes) now are:

- Sensitive, empathetic, and compassionate to anyone suffering

- Caring, understanding, and physically supportive of those in need

- Patient and non-judgmental of all persons

- Experienced at sharing our losses

- Prepared for life's shocks and challenges (practical, realists)

- Don't take things for granted in life (every day is precious)

- Tolerant of others who are different than ourselves

- Accepting of change for the better, always positively hopeful

- Resilient and resolute to living a great life personally

- Appreciative for life! *(We know that every day is a precious gift and it is an opportunity to help our fellowman and worship our God.)*

Those who have survived the suicide of a family member or friend still have questions (they still occur occasionally), but those who insist on living a full life have found a way to quell some of the questioning and move on. But, please don't ever look strangely at someone who has lived through the suicide of a loved one when they tell you so. Look with compassion and empathy, knowing what this person has already endured enough. Yes, express "I'm sorry you had to go through that". But also add a positive statement like "But I'm sure it has made you the strong person you are today" or simply a "God bless you" will suffice, and that survivor will appreciate your support, however minimal. If they express the need (or not) offer support through various agencies that you know are available *(see below),* or just offer to be able to talk with the person about it if/whenever they want to or offer them resources to help them heal. Give them your contact information if you're serious about that – you'd be surprised who would take you up on it. Tell them whether or not your parents are still living and that you will appreciate them *even more* since they're still available to you (if that is the case). If you have lost a parent (or any loved one) also to suicide, it's ok to share your loss too. Let them know (if you can empathize) that you feel the pain that they feel. Suicide occurs more often than we think in this country, and unfortunately *daily* in America many choose to sadly end their lives, impacting so many close families, friends, and all observers. They, for some reason, see this as a better option than life, some with clear intentions and others hiding what they plan to do. We can't always stop it, but *(per the Mayo Clinic)* we can try our best when we see the signs of "suicidal ideation" (someone thinking about suicide) in our loved ones:

- Withdrawal, not wanting to converse as often as normal

- Feeling trapped or hopeless about a situation

- Talk of "I want to die" or extreme statements like "I can't take this anymore"

- Change of normal routine: sleeping more, change of appetite

- Depressive state: listlessness, in a daze, always sad

- Stockpiling the tools used for self-destruction: pills, or buying a gun, etc.

- Giving their prize possessions away without explanation

- Saying goodbye to people or being overly affectionate (out of the normal)

- Developing personality changes: being anxious, nervous, and agitated, particularly when experiencing some of the other symptoms previously mentioned

If you or someone you know needs assistance, please encourage them to reach out to a loved one, a mental health professional, a member of the clergy, and/or one of the free services below to work their problems through.... Problems that seem suffocating at first, but really are always surmountable; they (or you) just can't see it and are blinded by depression or some other negative emotion. Never let that end your story. May God bless you and your family.

Call the **National Suicide Prevention Lifeline at 1-800-273-8255**.

OR

Call the **Trevor Project Lifeline at 1-866-488-7386**.

* * * * *

In spite of the great tragedy that had just occurred in our lives, we consistently have been blessed in many ways (group fashion and individually) ever since. Later in life as an adult, I sat down with one of my cousins, and he asked me while we were talking, "How do you all do it?" meaning me and my siblings. "Each of you are amazing people who have been through so much! And you're all so successful… each and every one of you!" I told my cousin that it is because we have positively persevered through our circumstances *together*. It has been through our unity, our faith, and our loving community – Angels all around – and from some sources we did not expect. We focus on these on-going in our lives, now with a greater understanding of our God-given purpose. We now try to be those "angels" for others.

My siblings and I surmounted this major tragedy in our lives together, but it was particularly hard for me being so young when it occurred. I, too, would not have made it through sanely without the verbal, spiritual, physical, and emotional support and daily assistance with my (our) daily living: from church (especially St. Mark), the community of Evanston (friends), and family (Kinneys and Robinsons). But there was one particular person in my Mom's life who stepped up during her major loss to help her (and us). She was *very* instrumental making life a bit more manageable for Mom during this particularly difficult time. Ironically, she would end up doing the exact same thing for me when I was in crisis years later. My "Auntie" has made a major impact on me and my siblings' lives... especially mine. After all, I am named after her...

Chapter 9:
Another Angel to the Rescue - "The Bird"

"And the multitude of them that believed were of one heart and of one soul; neither said of any of them that ought of the things which he possessed was his own; but they had all things in common. And with great power gave the apostles witness of the resurrection of the Lord Jesus; and great grace was up on them all. Neither was there any among them that lacked; for as many as were possessors of lands or houses sold them, and brought the prices of the things that were sold, and laid them down at the apostles' feet: and distribution was made unto every man according as he had need."
– Acts 4:32-35

Naomi Frazier was my mother's sister after who I am named. I was/am her "namesake", but did not like my name at first (sorry Auntie). I would give many other names when someone would ask me "What's your name, little girl?", and it angered my Mom to no end and was shameful to my Auntie. Once when the milkman came to deliver our weekly delivery of milk (remember those, in the foam-lined aluminum box that sat outside your front door?), I told him my name was "Geraldine" (remember Geraldine from the "Flip Wilson Show"?). Well, when my mother appeared to pay the bill, he stated "Your daughter, Geraldine, is beautiful!"

"What?!?!" my mother screamed angrily (not at the milkman, but glaring at me). "Her name is NOT Geraldine! It's Naomi!" "Well, that's much prettier!", yelled the milkman, giving me a puzzled look and backing away like "I'm not gonna get in the middle of this one!". I did not think that name was "much prettier", as Mom yanked me into the house and gave me a biblical lecture about the origin of my name. *(In case you don't know, in the book of Ruth in the Bible Naomi is the mother-in-law of Ruth, and they both suffer unimaginable losses. But it is a great story of perseverance and loyalty where Ruth tells Naomi "Entreat me not to leave thee or to return from following after thee; for whither thou goest I will go, and where thou lodgest, I will lodge. Thy people shall be my people, and thy God my God." - Ruth 1:16. It is a famous biblical quote that is often used in weddings across the nation.)*

My Aunt Naomi (or "Aunt Chick" as we all affectionately called her) was my mother's older sister and helpful right hand in raising her nine children after Mom abruptly became a widow in 1966. Aunt Chick took great delight in helping Mom and they were quite a team in making sure all of our needs were met over the years. With good sibling rivalry among them, she and Mom would occasionally vie for the attention of my grandmother/their mother ("Mother Rob"). My grandmother ("Mother Rob") on my mother's side of the family was a typical grandmother, doting over her grandchildren – something that Aunt Chick could not provide (she had no children), but my mother had an abundance of offspring to Mother Rob's delight. Each Sunday was a day set aside for family visits and gatherings, and we would go get our grandmother from her assisted living building in Avondale on Forest Avenue. Aunt Chick, who had a big black car, would go pick up Mother Rob and ask her "Momma, where do you want to go today?... To my house or to Freda's house?" Of course, she would opt to go where all the children were (our house), which proved to be upsetting for Aunt Chick sometimes. Aunt Chick would always end up bringing Mother Rob there and staying with us herself anyway, so I don't know why she would bother to ask her this question, knowing what Mother Rob's answer would be. Although Aunt Chick's place was only two blocks away (on the corner of Jonathan and Montgomery Avenue), Mother Rob didn't really want to sit up with Aunt Chick and her mean, alcoholic husband, Uncle Frazier (Howard was actually his first name, Frazier his last, but we still called him "Uncle Frazier"). He and Daddy actually used to have an occasional drink together.

Uncle Frazier made Aunt Chick's life miserable, at least we thought. But she still loved him to death, and doted over him constantly. All we saw was a guy who would sit in the kitchen by an open window overlooking the traffic on the newly constructed Highway I-71 below. He was often drunk (or just drinking coffee there), shouting out orders to Aunt Chick that she quickly obliged. When we visited she would tell us "Kiss your Uncle Frazier", and I would cringe and slowly approach to quickly kiss his cold, wet, clammy cheek. Sometimes he would get so drunk and could not get out of his car when he got home. So, Aunt Chick would call Mom to ask if two of her kids could help. When her boys were not available, Mom would send Angie and Ceal. Ceal later told me that he would be trying to "feel their titties" as they tried to drag him up the steps drunk to their second-floor apartment. She said she wished she could have just dropped him and left him on the street to sleep it off, but we all loved Aunt Chick too much to let that happen (knowing how much she loved him). She apparently needed our support as much as we needed hers.

Once when "Auntie" was five months pregnant, he pushed her down the steps of their apartment building in one of his drunken angry rages, and she lost her baby that day. She also lost the ability to have other children. This history between them was yet another reason for us to turn our nose up to Uncle Frazier every time we saw him. Years later gangrene formed in his left leg (being diabetic), and he had to have that leg amputated, curbing his runs back and forth to the local bars and the liquor store. For some reason, after that he stopped drinking, actually went to church with Aunt Chick (something she would traditionally do solo or drag some of us along), and he started being much nicer to us and to Aunt Chick as well (which I know she saw as a blessing). We all thought "well, it's about time!" Too bad that it took all that in life for him to get there, especially for her sake.

With no children to care for of her own, she slowly realized that we were her children and that God had put the charge before her to help her sister (my mother) to raise us. And that she did in a very committed fashion. I remember many nights having to go to Aunt Chick's house to eat dinner, because we had nothing in our cabinets. And my Mom would often send just us three youngest (Cynthia, Carl, and myself) to make sure we ate well. While there, Aunt Chick would make us wash every dish we used, and had additional tasks for us to do while there (it's like she kept a list and pulled it out when we arrived… always lots to do there in her small apartment). I am eternally grateful to Aunt Chick for all of those nights of support and many others that she provided to my mother, her sister. I later felt guilty about wanting to possess another name; Naomi was a name that is truly honorable and my aunt displayed this regularly as we were raised there in Evanston.

A child of the Depression, she taught us never to waste anything, introducing me to rummage sales and garage sales to buy things at a discount. Once Cindy, Carl, and I were in the car with her coming back from a trip to Twin Fair, and we all discovered a pile of what looked like brand-new socks in the middle of the road on Dana Avenue. Aunt Chick turned around with the intent to get the socks, and when we got up on them, it was for sure three brand new pairs of socks that looked like they fell out of someone's car in transit. Aunt Chick demanded "Cindy, go over there and pick up those socks so I can take them to Freda. She got them boys; they could use those socks." Cindy was mortified, mouth hanging open from the shock of asking her to do that, and did not budge. Auntie did not send me or Carl, because she did not want to put children in the street in the middle of Dana Avenue. So, she put her car in park, and she herself carefully stepped out in traffic to pick up those new socks! And yes, she brought them to Grantwood, and gave them to Mom(where Fran and Chico probably did not know the difference of where those socks came from).

Aunt Chick would take one, two, or three plates of leftovers from her church gatherings, events where she worked, or from any other place across Cincinnati with some "extras", and would bring those "extras" right over to Grantwood where there were always lots of hungry mouths to feed. And we would gobble it up! She would often drop through after church and pop the "magical" trunk of her big black four-door car, and boy, the wondrous things that would come out of that trunk! And it seemed like she would arrive just when we were really hungry and the cupboards were bare! My brothers tell the story to this day about her driving by our house one day (while they were out front playing football in the middle of Grantwood as they often did), and Aunt Chick had to work one of the elegant parties held by her affluent Jewish employer where they served caviar and smoked salmon on crackers. Fran and Chico told me that they were SO hungry that day, and there came Aunt Chick into the middle of our black neighborhood, offering those leftover caviar and lox on crackers! It's a riot to hear my brother tell this story about how every opportunity she could she nourished us, but often it was with the VERY best cuisine! ⏃ To this day, we call her attitude of being thrifty "Chickism". So, every time we're taking an extra plate from somewhere, every time we hoard leftover ketchup packets from eating out ("There's still a lot of good ketchup in there!" she'd say), every time we put something in a cup to eat it, we look at one another and say, "Chickism", and smile.

As all nine of us grew up under that one roof on Grantwood Avenue in Evanston with our amazing single Mom, there is story after story of us having fun together, fighting, going through our daily routines together, and each individually coming into our own adulthood while Aunt Chick was right there on the periphery sharing these wonderful times with us. We had very busy Saturday afternoons doing chores and preparing for Sunday church, and then the fabulous Sunday family dinners the next day allowed us all to gather (often with other family members included) to get an update on what everyone had been doing during the week. That Sunday evening, we could all be found either doing our homework, preparing our uniforms to attend St. Mark School the next day, or watching "The Wonderful World of Disney" Sunday evening programming together on our one television set. Sometimes Mother Rob would cut on the "Lawrence Welk Show", and we all could clear the room! Our house never had a dull moment with nine kids around, and all my friends and cousins wanted to join in on our "special place on Grantwood" where all this loving magic took place. We had fun playing games in the short street we lived on along with the other kids in the neighborhood, until the street light came on and you had to come in (that was the rule). But some nights we all were allowed to stay out late if we were involved in good game of Red Light, Green Light. We had a close-knit relationship with all our neighbors on that street like they were family. And everyone knew that "Aunt Chick" would ride through at any moment, pop her trunk, and share with anyone all the magical, delicious, useful things she had stored there. It was truly "a village" and a great environment to grown up in as I reminisce.

At Easter and Christmas time we had wonderful family gatherings inviting other family members in, and on those occasions our house was packed! Aunt Chick would go pick up Mother Rob so they both could join us too after they would attend Bethlehem Baptist church in Avondale, where she took us every summer for Vacation Bible School ("so those kids can have something to do over the summer"). The night before Easter, Mom would work all night to sew together our outfits for church the following day. When we would wake on Easter morning, Mom would surprise us with two huge baskets loaded with candy, and we all would devour all the candy before the end of the day. At Christmas, we would manage to get lots of Christmas gifts under the tree for all of us (9 x 9 meant a loaded Christmas tree!). It was a joyous time when we would string popcorn to put on our tree, but had a dog named "Timmy" (after Rinney died) who would try to eat it, making the whole tree come down. We would have to get it standing up again repeatedly. When I was a little girl I used to draw pictures with my crayons for my siblings for Christmas, something that probably drove them crazy like the many other wacky things their little sister did. I also remember the Christmas when we got robbed, discovered when we returned from Midnight Mass at St. Marks Church. My sister's accused the crooked buddies of Chico and Fran, but we never found out who did it. I remember Mom made us all stand there and pray for those who stole from us! We have so many good holiday memories of our times together as a family on Grantwood, even though Daddy was not with us anymore and not in the picture.

Mom, Aunt Chick, and "Mother Rob" – short for Robinson (their mother, my grandmother) always led the charge with lots of cooking, making the house fill with the aroma of home-cooked food, telling us all what to do to prepare the house for guests, and welcoming of anyone we would have at our family gatherings. I also have great memories of LOTS of birthday parties for me and my siblings. I remember one party for me (I must have been about 7 years old), and it had a carnival theme. We had little card tables set up around our living room and adjoining dining room as well as on the front porch, where me and my friends could go from station to station playing games and winning prizes. My siblings manned all the "booths". It was SO much fun! My siblings always doted over me being the youngest, and I loved it! I now realize that not only did my Mom, Aunt Chick (who lived two blocks away), and "Mother Rob" protect me, but definitely my siblings protected me. There was talk of "don't mess with her; that's Chico's or Angie's little sister... you'll have to contend with ALL the Kinneys if you do!"

But Mom and Aunt Chick had a solid relationship that focused on us kids and all of our needs being met. My other Robinson aunts and uncles, particularly, did the same knowing Mom had a full house. I remember once Uncle Bill pulled up to our house with a new washing machine for Mom from the Jewish family he worked with (it seemed like the Jewish families often supported our Black families, and that was nice to see), and other times he would bring furniture or lamps. But Mom and Aunt Chick specifically, worked together like a team on everything (probably considered common at the time then for Black families to merge resources across the community). However, their spirited debates ensued about "Momma" (Mother Rob) wanting to go to our house more than to her apartment each week. The fact that Mom named one of her children after her said a lot about their relationship, and now I am proud to bear her name. But I now realize that Mom gave her something she could not have: a child, and one with her name. And now I know why Aunt Chick doted over me for years, calling me "namesake" at every chance she could. Back then many families on the block and even our cousins and their families grew to admire our household and how we all kept it together over the years with so much functionality, so much love, closeness, and fun. They also all knew about the key role that "Aunt Chick" played in our family, and she got greetings from everyone in the neighborhood accordingly, knowing her lifeline connection to our big family. Our home life and family was irresistible and gravitating to many.

(Like all our other monikers, Uncle "Bill", her brother, gave Naomi Frazier the name "Chick" and is also known by him as "The Bird". He said it was because of how much she talked. And she definitely liked to talk!)

Chapter 10:
Angels All Around Me

And God shall wipe away all tears from their eyes; and there shall be no more death, neither sorrow, nor crying, neither shall there be any more pain: for the former things are passed away.
– Revelations 21:4

I am Naomi, the baby of the family. I'll be 90 years old and my dear siblings will still refer to me as "the baby of the family". ☺ I was born in 1963 during very turbulent times in America and more specifically in my neighborhood of Evanston in Cincinnati, Ohio. Like Carl, I was one of Sissy and Buddy's "blondie" children that received regular teasing from the kids in the neighborhood because of it. I was called names like "Casper the Friendly Ghost", "Yellow Banana", and "Goldilocks", some I found offensive and some things funny. And like Carl, sometimes my siblings would tease me about the size of my head, singing to me "Pumpkin head, Neomi, Neomi, Neomi!" So, we talked about each other's features in fun, because we all had physical features so unique to our individual selves.

But when I stepped out of the house (all through my life), I came to realize that I was going to get flack from both the white community and the black community (like Daddy) because of my appearance, having green eyes (that sometimes change colors with the seasons), reddish-brown hair, and fair skin. I also have the nerve to have a mole right between my eyes that some have blatantly tried to wipe off my face as if it were makeup. This mole makes my appearance even more unique, and it often makes people do a double-take and look at me closer, I've noticed. My looks always made me stand out among the other kids.

I grew up admiring, mimicking, and following the learnings of my 8 older siblings, which gave me a great vantage point in life. I tried to be athletic, smart, productive, and capable just like they all were (are). I reveled in playing board games with them, competing to see who is most clever and smart, while laughing together. Besides chasing after Carl (my constant best buddy), when I was a young girl, I played often with my best friend Deneen Robinson (who lived down the street on Grantwood with her big family – it was her father who was with Mr. Jackson when they found Daddy). We would play jacks together, tether ball, and any other games the kids in the neighborhood had going in the middle of Grantwood. I remember she taught me how to tie my shoes and how to strike a match, something we were not supposed to be playing with). We would ride our bikes all over the neighborhood, looking for adventures or to stop by Miss Mamie Beal's house on Dauner Avenue to get candy (she always had some!). Once we were riding our bikes up Clarewood (just a block over from Grantwood), and we heard a band playing live music. We got off our bikes and started dancing in front of the house where the music was playing. Those inside noticed, and came out onto the top porch. One of those I recognized immediately by the big pompadour style front to his afro: "Sugarfoot" (Leroy Bonner) and the Ohio Players were inside practicing! We laughed, waved at them, got back on our bikes, and kept rolling through the `hood. I later found out that lots of musical talent came out of Ohio even after the notoriety of King Records. Evanston was truly a special place, and an incubator, of amazing talent.

Deneen continued to hang with me in my youth, in my obsession with games, puzzles, and riddles; I was always trying to solve a problem (in school or at home). She would also join me in my obsession of tetherball, volleyball, and roller skating as we grew up. I was always into school and loved academics, always a straight-A student. Much to his chagrin, I was placed in Carl's 8th grade English class by Mrs. Burke (a teacher at St. Mark), because I was so advanced and wrote so well (later Mrs. Burke introduced me to Spanish in 8th grade at St. Mark).

I was very intelligent as a child, because after all, I had eight siblings to follow after and watch constantly. So, I took full advantage of that, learning what to do more of *and* what not to do at all. I was often the center of attention of my siblings, always the one being picked up, kissed and hugged, and to have fun with being the smallest. I was the one who was always allowed to eat *first* before all the others (as at dinner time my Mom would yell "babies first!" to allow me, Carl, and Cindy to be first in line to eat before my older siblings took their bigger servings). I had a blessed childhood being the youngest of nine children; so many challenging, funny, interesting, and loving moments among us.

My mother once told me that she was holding me in her arms as a baby while she watched Dr. Martin Luther King, Jr. give his "I Have a Dream" speech. It was a turbulent time in America and also in the small community of Evanston where we grew up; it was actually a hot-bed of racially-driven activity at the time. I was under the misconception (as a child) that I was living in a sweet, peaceful community that was not necessarily poor, had many close families, and it felt (it was) safe. On the contrary, there were a lot of other very dangerous and yet exciting activities going on in Cincinnati (some nearby) that I never knew about when I was young. But I was enlightened on much of this, ironically, after I left Cincinnati for college and into my adult life. I kept learning more and more interesting things about the history of my hometown and about my family persevering through all this.

Our upbringing was precious... All nine of us together and my Mom amazingly living together stuffed into that house at 1607 Grantwood, fights, scuffles, and all. And I often felt like the center of attention (along with Carl, since we were the youngest). When I look at the house, still standing today, it's hard to believe that 9 children grew up there. That address and street name rings in our hearts to this day and is a sacred place where a lot of interesting memories transpired. We played music on Daddy's Hi-Fi stereo and danced together there, played lots of fun games together pressing our sibling rivalry and competition even further, we fought and suffered our punishments there (I remember us having to "stand in the corner" for long periods when we acted out), and we had many family celebrations, meals, holidays, and gatherings together there on Grantwood. We even got in trouble *together*, our initial tests of teamwork. I recall one occasion when my Mom had prepared a large German chocolate cake, and stored it in our refrigerator for someone's birthday. Later when Mom looked in at it, a huge gouge had been taken out of the cake! So, Mom lined us ALL us in the living room, and we all had to stand there (for what seemed like hours) until someone came clean on who ate the cake. We started in on each other, and everyone was looking at and blaming me or Carl, the youngest! We later found out that darling little Cindy was the culprit, but we all had to suffer extra chores, no allowance, and a bunch of other sanctions that Mom put on us for that incident. But even being so young, I have memories of us standing for so long in the living room, suffering together, and pressing one another to resolve the issue (and ironically, we still kind of do that to this day). Now, we still work together to resolve issues, but now we know how to do so a bit more lovingly with better communication.

As were grew up together, I was the precocious, busy, curious little one who was always in everyone else's business, trying to learn everything from my siblings, much to their annoyance. I would roam around our house at Grantwood just searching to join in on whatever my siblings were doing (until I later gained my own interests... learning new facts was big on my list). Carl and I would sit for hours and read through the World Book Encyclopedia set that my Mom wisely purchased for us, fascinated by the images and information that we saw in there... we were both really *very* smart kids and challenged each other constantly in this regard, which only made us smarter. I was always trying to join in one of my brothers' sports games in front of the house (football or basketball), and next would frolic in the kitchen and join in with my Mom and my sisters preparing meals for our large family.

I, too, got in my share of trouble with Mom, always in competition with my siblings for what we had in the house. (You surely could never "hide" anything in our refrigerator!) Once Mom received a huge heart-shaped box of assorted chocolate candies for Valentine's Day from a family friend who knew she would be sharing them with her many children. Well, I wanted those chocolates so bad... and I wanted them *all* just for me! So, I proceeded to lock myself in Mom's bedroom that was on the first floor of the house with the chocolates, eating as many as I could as quickly as I could. When Mom came knocking on the door, knowing why I was in there, she became angry, and then she stormed outside the house, banging on the windows of her bedroom from the outside to get my attention; she could see me inside gobbling up the chocolates in rapid fashion, watching her try to get in. When she noticed her youngest daughter's defiant look, she quickly ran around to our bulkhead door in the back of the house that led to the basement utility room. She jumped up on the closed steel bulkhead doors, opened the window (while I was watching her, too dumb to lock the window, and stuffing candy into my mouth as fast as I could dreading that she would eventually reach me before I finished them all). I've never seen Mom move so acrobatically before, but she opened that window and jumped through (with a dress on), knocked over her sewing machine in the corner while doing so, snatched the candy out of my hands, and then snatched me also in rapid fashion! Boy, did I get a butt-whooping to remember after that, had to stand in the corner quietly for a bit (typical punishment among me and my siblings then), and was grounded for a few days too!

Back then, life on Grantwood was truly idyllic. We all would ride our bikes around the neighborhood barefoot without a worry or care in the world. If we were not running back and forth to Jonathan Park (a place we still treasured in spite of its history), we were right in the middle of Grantwood Avenue itself trying to think of a kid's game that all of us neighborhood kids could participate in such as "Red-light, Green-light" or "Hide and Seek." The summers brought with it a lot of hair braiding, desires of going swimming at the neighborhood Evanston Community Recreation Center, and doing our daily chores at home before Mom returned from work at the end of the day. I remember she would give me/us a dollar for a carton of eggs for everyone to share for the day before she would leave. We ate a lot more eggs than meat when my Mom was trying to stretch her budget. So, me and my siblings would get creative with meals when the cupboards begin to bare, making things like popcorn, peanut butter and jelly or grilled cheese sandwiches (Aunt Chick would get us the huge can of USDA peanut butter and a block of cheese occasionally), or cinnamon toast and tea. So, our summer months proved to be a bit hungrier than most with nine children in the house, but families in the neighborhood often fed each other's children. So, if we were hungry, we would hit a friend's house nearby. Somebody was always cooking something on Grantwood. We even had a garden in the back of our yard at one time. It was on the back rear corner of our house just behind the garage, and it was positioned right next to our neighbor, Mr. Brown's intricate grape vines (the other family with the name Brown in our neighborhood). It is hard to believe now that we had grapes growing right in the middle of Evanston at that time, and they were delicious. In the summers, our five cherry trees out front would burst with fruit, and we had to guard it from the neighborhood kids, tying Wrennie to the base of the tree to be an alarm of sorts. We had all kinds of things growing around our house, which sometimes seemed lacking and other times seemed overly abundant. We all went with the flow on either occasion, learning that our trying times were always temporary.

I also treasured hanging out and playing with my young cousins growing up as a young girl. Rocky (Raymond Jr.) and Lisa were born to my mother's other brother Ray Robinson, Sr, and they were about the same age as me and my brother Carl. Uncle Ray worked for the U.S. Postal Service and Aunt Hazel (his wife) was a nurse. So Rocky, Lisa, and their little sister Joanne (who we called "Joey") all did pretty well, living in the more affluent College Hill area of Cincinnati. We would visit them regularly in the summer time, and Uncle Ray would fix our bikes so they would run well and we would have something to play with in front of their house on the cul de sac. He was always fixing or working on someone's bike or lawnmower (from the neighborhood) in his basement where there were at least 5 or 6 bikes stored there at a time. And Aunt Hazel kept Lisa, Rocky, and Joey under strict supervision while giving them everything they needed and more. I admired their household, how with 1/3 the number of kids we had they had so much more to go around to everyone in their house, and how they often wore new clothes and shoes (I remember wearing a lot of hand-me-downs from my sisters often and I didn't have my own bed until I was about 9 – we shared everything in our house on Grantwood). I loved spending the afternoon with Rocky and Lisa in College Hill to see a matinee movie nearby or join them at their Baptist Church services on Sunday the following day when we would stay a weekend. But ironically, Rocky, Lisa, and Joey always longed to come to *our* busy house with all the people to experience all the fun and love going on among me and my siblings on Grantwood in Evanston. It's amazing the interesting perspectives and values of children back then.

In the winters full of snow (sometimes blizzards) in Cincinnati in the early 60's, my siblings and I would take our sleds up to St. Mark Church and use the hill on the back lot behind the school to sleigh the day away when school was out due to snow. We had a long toboggan sled that held at least three of us (I was always safely cushioned in the middle between my older siblings as we rode it to keep me safe). We also had a few of those silver round saucers that you ride individually. And one of my older siblings always had to go with us to make sure that we all stayed safe while out sledding and did not stay out too long. In all the fun, we sometimes could forget that it's freezing cold, and we often came home with cheeks rosy from the cold trying to endure it as long as we could so that we could have one more slide. A group of us would go up to St. Mark's knocking on doors as we go, letting the other neighborhood kids know of our plans for sledding the steep hill on the rear side of St. Mark's church parking lot. On the snowy hill you had to steer your sled just right to avoid hitting a row of trees off to the left, but if you did it right, it was always a really good, long and fast sleigh ride. I remember trying to take in all the beauty of the heavy falling snow and how everything was so white and pristine during these winters. My Robinson cousins would visit us in winter often during their school breaks and join us sleighing as well, and they would join us when we did Christmas caroling through Evanston, which St. Mark's children's choir initiated (and was overseen by Father Kinderman). We had great family fun and family traditions, all tied into our faith at the beloved St. Mark, where we were always told how special we were (are) regardless of our race or position in life.

Like Rocky and Lisa, Diane and David Robinson (cousins from West End) would have overnights with us to do just the same. Diane and David are two of eleven children by my mother's bother Charles "Gus" and Mary Robinson. We would visit their house on Thanksgiving, and Aunt Mary would have a feast prepared for all her many children in a kitchen even smaller than ours. I used to be amazed at how she would make six or more pies from scratch and have them ready with all the other Thanksgiving food available. Aunt Mary sure would throw down cooking as could my mom. It's amazing as I look back on our families and realize how my parents, aunts, and uncles actually worked as a team to take care of all of us at that time... to make sure we all had what we needed. They all worked together as a village to care for us all, the very young children growing up in Cincinnati's Black community in the mid-60s.

My Mom was just an *amazing* woman. Besides having 9 kids within 11 years' time and raising them on her own. She was quite the leader in her family *and* in her local community. She was the President of the Evanston block club for a while, and held the meetings at our house. She would set out her punch bowl and snacks for the meetings, and we could not wait to attack as soon as they left. She was the head of our household, combatted the challenges of my older siblings, managed the financial needs of the house, and even shooed the bats out of our house that would occasionally fly into an upstairs window if we left it open at night. Mom was also the ultimate seamstress, and taught all of us how to sew. We also all stood in as a model if Mom needed to cut out a pattern on the dining room table (the only time I was ever allowed to stand on a table in our house). Weeks before Easter Sunday, she would not only make dresses for all her daughters (in different pastel colors that we all hate to this day), but she would also make dresses and outfits for her nieces and nephews. Mom even had my Uncle Bill on the sewing machine since he was really into dressing up and looking "clean" in his colorful, stylish outfits. And in the summer time, she would go and visit my father's brother George Kinney and his wife Aunt Kathleen in Lansing, Michigan, where she could relax and get away from the kids for a bit. She would always come back looking so copper tan and beautifully rested, only temporary until she got back to mothering.

I had no idea that those years while living on Grantwood would rush by like a flash in my mind. After attending eight years at St. Mark Elementary School (like most of my siblings), I graduated in 1977 and was off to high school. Having followed all eight of my siblings around, watching and learning everything that they did (some good and some bad), I became very smart and kept on getting straight A's in school. I also wanted to look past the stigma of suicide and death that had shrouded our family, and I wanted to move onto a new era of "The Kinneys - the Wise Ones" instead. Many of my other siblings attended Catholic high schools, matriculating well in the 1970s. After St. Mark, I attended Ursuline Academy of Cincinnati that was close to 20 miles from my home in Blue Ash (I took two buses to get there and did the same to get home each school day). None of my other siblings had gone there, but Cindy would join me later (as Regina High School in Norwood had closed). We had a little financial support at this time, my Mom being the head of household now. I have no idea how Mom parlayed paying for *both* of us to attend that elite school (especially for Cindy's last two years of high school). This was the time of my life when running with my friends Deneen and Monica Berry (who also grew up on Grantwood across the street) to the local Royale skating rink for some good, clean fun. It was the one place my Mom let me go to and didn't worry too much about me (except for the one time she surprised me and showed up at the rink amazed that I could skate so well). She later began to trust me a bit more going out as a young teen.

During my 7th and 8th grades, Sr. Rose Helene arranged that I give my Mom a break and attend the summer camp in St. Martins, Ohio which is run by the Ursulines of Brown County. They ran a boarding school there, and in the summer, it became an all-girls summer camp, full of religious study and activity nestled in the beautiful wooded campus with the long tree-lined driveway entrance (I'll never forget that long driveway and the peacefulness and beauty of the main chapel there). The faces I saw here I would eventually see again in months to come who also were so nice to me. They taught me something every time I saw them, and made sure my faith stayed strong. These beautiful faces include: Sr. Phyllis Kemper, Sr. Ellen Doyle, Sr. MaryAnn Janssen, and Sr. Cecilia Huber. Thank God that these women of faith looked beyond my skin-color and saw something in me that I did not see in myself at the time (academically, spiritually, and just as a promising young woman).

When it was time to decide on high schools, I figured I would naturally follow my sisters' footsteps and go to Marian High School in Madisonville (where Ceal went) or go to St. Ursula Academy in nearby Walnut Hills. So, when I was in the 8th grade ready to graduate from St. Mark, and was asked "Where are you going to high school?", I would name these schools. Well, when that question came up in the presence of Sr. Rose Helene, she firmly but sweetly said to me "Oh no! You're not going there with your grades; you're going to Ursuline Academy!" I asked, "Where is that at?" And she replied, "In Blue Ash – it's a way's away, but you can take a bus to get there." Just before I graduated from St. Mark, she took me to Blue Ash to take the test to go to Ursuline Academy. And although I passed the exam, scoring at sophomore knowledge level, it was Sr. Rose Helene Wildehaus who still had to convince the administration to permit both me and my sister Cynthia (and two other girls from St. Mark) to attend the elite school. Then my mother hit me with the news that I could not attend Ursuline Academy unless I got a scholarship; she did not have the tuition money – another barrier. Well,

Sr. Rose Helene, working in tandem with my eighth-grade math teacher (Mrs. Brenda Warner Madison) got busy and found me some scholarship money to go to Ursuline Academy! I remember racing home to give Mom the news after school, and she had to say "well, it looks like you're going to Ursuline Academy!" I was elated! And when I found out Cindy, Stephanie Mayfield, and Tammy Daniels (other St. Mark girls who were Cindy's close friends from Regina High School in nearby Norwood that was closing, like many Catholic schools nationwide) would be going with me too to finish her high school years, that was very cool too. I graduated from St. Mark in 1977, and this is right when Mom started getting very ill. She was going in and out of the hospital in my early high school years, and it was something I just got used to.

I am very thankful to Sr. Rose Helene and Father Kinderman (rector/priest) for being behind my entire family, particularly as we grew up after the death of my father. And now thinking back, I believe they both knew that Mom was becoming seriously ill, but not letting me know that until I absolutely had to. Life in the Kinney house was never a dull moment for me for sure, and being the youngest I received a LOT of love, care, and affection from all my siblings as we grew up on Grantwood. But that changed when they started leaving the nest moving on with their own lives, and it eventually became just Mom and me on Grantwood.

Being one of a few Black students at this school (2% at the time), I was nervous about showing up for orientation at Ursuline Academy, but lo and behold – who do I see at orientation? - Sr. Phyllis Kemper and Sr. Ellen Doyle from Ursuline Camp in Brown County, Ohio! Seeing their familiar faces brought me much comfort in my first few weeks at Ursuline Academy. They would always stop and ask me "How's it going, Naomi?" with much genuine interest. My work at that school was rigorous academically, but I reveled in that being so smart and competitive (and looking back really needed that at the time to occupy my mind for all that was going on). I also had to contend with many racial comments I received at school ("You don't belong here!" and "Why don't your clothes match colors, Naomi?" Our uniform allowed us to wear solid colors, so many of the girls wore colorful button-down collared shirts with Izod or Polo logos on them with matching socks. I was concerned with just getting to school in a clean shirt and socks each day… it was not a fashion show for me!). I always felt lots of competition at Ursuline, but was used to this being the youngest of nine kids, so I was ready for it. But my image as a young black woman was at stake here, and so I always felt pressured to be the best I could be, knowing I really represented *all* Black people to my fellow classmates there. For some of them, I was their only real-life example to go by, and I wanted to always make that a positive impression that they would have on me (and my people). But I had so many great classmates that made my experience there wonderful considering all that was occurring in my young life (many I stay in touch with to this day e.g., Robin, Tanya, Lana, Lauren, Michelle, Tammy, Sandra, Mary, and many others). I knew Robin (who is black) from St. Mark, but of all my friends black and white that I've had at Ursuline, it's Tammy (who is white) who greeted me freshman year with the sweetest smile, introducing herself boldly "Hi, I'm Tammy!" I'll never forget that sweet day in high school. It would be the beginning of a long-cherished friendship.

But while matriculating at Ursuline, I did not get all of the pleasures of high school that my classmates got, for going through so much personally in my homelife, being a care-giver for Mom, and working at Skyline Chili. I never got the chance to go to prom, a typical rite of passage of most high school students. I never went to any of the dances, because I never had money to buy nice outfits to wear. I never had the transportation to get all the way out to the school after hours (where most of the dances were held), and I never dated boys (for fear of getting pregnant, something I saw some of my friends in Evanston doing that would have been disastrous for me at that time. I know my siblings were dreading that too). I never got to attend any of the "Father-Daughter Dances" or the "Mother-Daughter Tea Parties" that Ursuline Academy offered each year, and dreaded anyone asking me "Are you going to go? Why not?" I didn't want to discuss any issues regarding my par-ents with anyone. I could not afford to get a class ring or a class jacket like my classmates, and again did not even want to talk with them about any of those things, for fear of making me feel worse or less than in their eyes. I just quietly buckled down, and focused on my school work, trying not to be noticed among my affluent classmates.

(Years later as adults at one of our UA class reunions, my classmate Sandra Melia-Usleman found out about me not getting a class ring and why. She surprisingly gave me hers! I love you forever for that, girl! All my UA classmates are gems!)

My mother developed a lung fungus called pulmonary sarcoidosis. During this time while at home, my Mom kept a bucket next to her bed to spit in when she would get into her coughing bouts, some worse than others. I would hear her from upstairs coughing and coughing in the middle of the night. After a while it was just she and I in the house, and sometimes she would call my name really early in the morning as she struggled to stop coughing. Sometimes she woke me up at 5am to make her one fried egg over easy to ease her hunger. I would ask "Mom, don't you want two eggs? Do you want some toast or something else?", but she would always tell me "No... just one fried egg over easy, baby, with a little salt and pepper." It was irritating for me to have to wake up early and care for my Mom *before* my busy, demanding school day began at Ursuline; but my older siblings and my Aunt Chick who lived nearby would stop by later in the afternoon to care for her to take some of the burden off me. But when they returned to their homes, and I returned home from work in the evening, it was just me and Mom, and that awful illness that eventually overtook her breathing capabilities. She eventually had to get an oxygen tank and lug it around the house with her, which we both tried to avoid for her sake. So, I handled most of the tasks around the house to meet her needs in between family members and friends dropping by. After experiencing Mom going in and out of the hospital repeatedly all year long because of this lung fungus (Mom smoked, but not much) in 1979 Mom went into the hospital on Christmas Day and never came out this time. Being so young, I will never forget how angry I felt that my Christmas was taken away from me, but then my focus eventually turned to my dying mother when she never came home. She was eventually transitioned to Drake Memorial Hospital and Rehabilitation Center north of Cincinnati, where they also took my grandmother Jewel Robinson (her mother). So, as a 16-year-old I went to visit both my Mom *and* my maternal grandmother at the same time at this nursing home (hospice center) twice a week. It was heart-breaking and depressing, especially knowing where this was all headed. I kept asking myself "When that occurs, what the hell is going to happen to me?"

Dear "Mother Rob" died in spring of 1980, and Mom's death came soon after in June (grandmother Kinney died six months after that too). The Ursuline Academy staff was incredibly supportive of me during my mother's illness, allowing me to get counseling from our caring priest at the time (a Father Jeff Kemper), and even allowing him to take me to Drake nursing center to see Mom where she had been convalesced (ironically, alongside her mother, Mother Rob). If I wanted to go see Mom in the middle of the class, I was given permission to tell the teacher that I needed to go the office, and there they would notify Fr. Jeff Kemper. He would come immediately, we would get in his car, and drive to Drake Hospital where I could see Mom for as long as I needed to. But this also meant that all my teaching staff at UA had to have been told of my situation, and were working together for me to get the support and help I needed at the time. I am eternally grateful to him (and the staff) for responding to my needs like that in my mother's last days. *(Later in my adulthood decades later, I found out that Sr. Phyllis Kemper and Fr. Jeff Kemper are actually brother and sister. **Look at God!** They, too, and many in my Ursuline Academy family taught me early on that color does not matter when we are caring for our fellow man or woman. "We are our brother's and sister's keepers" - regardless of race, religion, or status.)*

One day at Ursuline at the end of my junior year while Mom was still at Drake, I was called to the principal's office. Mrs. Shirley Speakes told me "Naomi, we know you've gone through a lot recently with your mother's illness. Our Academic Advisory Committee has heard about your situation." I thought at first, that I was in trouble. Then she said, "You're not a problem student at all; we have no disciplinary issues with you. And your academic record is really good. So, knowing your situation, we all have agreed to pay for your senior year's tuition at Ursuline Academy." I leaned over and cried on that woman's desk right then and there, previously not knowing how on earth I was going to pay for my Senior year with my mother dying! A huge amount of relief came over me to know that I could stay with the same rigorous academic program, my same friends (especially my friends Robin and Tammy), and I could finish and complete my diploma at this prestigious school like my other classmates after having worked hard here for three years (and knowing how hard Sr. Rose Helene had worked for me to get into this school). I went home from school that day loving the fact that I attended Ursuline Academy, and feeling good that they cared enough to take that level of compassionate action on my behalf. *(Again, look at God working in my life! I obviously have many "angels" watching over me.)*

Two days later after receiving that good news from Ursuline Academy, on June 8th, 1980, I received some other startling news. I was working at Skyline Chili the restaurant job my three sisters before me had held and passed along to one another as we matured. My junior year at Ursuline had ended, and I would be working there at Skyline for the summer to make money. I received a call at the restaurant. Maple, the lady who supervised me for that shift and worked with me as a server at Skyline, answered the phone. She shouted that it was for me, and I grabbed the phone in work mode, thinking it was a call-in order to be taken. When I got on the phone, I heard my sister Cindy, and she rattled off to me over many tears that our dear, young mother of 45 had just passed away in the nursing home (only months after her mother had died in the same place!). With customers in front of me waiting for their chili orders to be taken/rung out, I froze, holding the telephone to my ear as the news sunk in and registered in my mind. I was devastated, crushed, and shocked... I could not move. I knew this day would come, but was this really happening here and now and like this in front of all these people?!?! Maple called my name to the back of my head for what must have been five times, before she realized something was wrong. Then I turned, she saw my face, and she sighed for all to hear, "Oh my God, your mother!" I dropped the phone, and I dashed to the back of the restaurant crying to get out of the view of the customers present, who were probably also asking themselves "what just happened?" (Something bad, I think.)

Someone had to come and get me from the restaurant. I don't even remember who that was who came and got me then, but in about 20 minutes I was headed to the Avondale section of Cincinnati to Cindy's apartment (then) to meet up with my siblings who were all in tears all over one another when I arrived. This was a very, very, very sad day for me and my siblings... now **both** of our parents were deceased. And we all had to come to grips of closing down 1607 Grantwood, our childhood home. My Mom sold our home on Grantwood before her death, knowing that she was not going to be here very long, and she even helped plan her own funeral. She even left me and my brother a small inheritance for college. But it was a devastating time for me as a young teenage girl having lost her only parent; I was stunned. Although I had a huge family, I felt so alone in the world. I was numb, in a daze constantly asking myself "What now?" and "What the heck?" But praise God that I had a lot of wonderful people around me, knowing my potential and encouraging me to keep going instead of stalling like I felt like doing. My other siblings were adults, out of college, having children, and/or just working... I was the only one still under-aged when Mom died. Wow... double-whammy: seventeen with NO parents.... An **orphan**. I started thinking that God forgot about me when he was giving out blessings. "What a mean, cruel, and unfair world!" I thought often at that time. I was very, *very* angry at everyone (God included), and felt like I really had been dealt a bad hand in life. But I was yet to understand my purpose.

I remember when Mrs. Shirley Gaede Speakes (principal of Ursuline Academy) and Sr. Regina Winters (my pottery teacher) showed up at my Mom's funeral. I was a mess, and it was then, I think, that they realized the gravity of the pain and suffering one of their students was experiencing... they knew I needed help. They have seen many intelligent young women go through Ursuline Academy with nice, wholesome, wealthy and well-supported families with both parents always present.... That was NOT the case with this young promising UA student that they saw in front of them crying her eyes out, distraught with anger.

They had driven the 20 miles from Blue Ash down into the small community of Evanston (the "hood") to support one of their students during her loss, and walked up on the scene after the service had started. I was standing on the porch of St. Mark Church (the place of my mom's funeral), being held by my brother Bobby as I cried my eyes out. I was having a tantrum right there in front of St. Mark Church. Ten minutes earlier the funeral had started. My mom's body (in a closed casket) was laying in state in the side vestibule of the church in front of the statue of Mother Mary (something they rarely did in Catholic churches). I had run past that statue many times as a kid in church and knelt and prayed right before Mother Mary for many supplications. I was still kneeling before her casket under the statue when the service started and I was eventually the only one left over there in front of the casket praying solo. Bobby saw me and came over to get me to try to bring me back over to the pews and join the service. I couldn't move. I thought "If I stay here, I can still be as close to her as possible until they take her away. I'll just stay right here." I wanted to stay as close to Mom as possible until she was gone out of my life for good.

Bobby knelt next to me, praying with me for a minute, then he whispered in my ear, "Come on, sis, let's go and sit down with the family." I said "No" quietly and curtly at first, but several times he gently tugged on my arms. Finally, he gently put his arm around me as if he were hugging me, but instead he lifted me up completely and "walked" me toward the back of the church. As he firmly but sweetly pulled me away from the casket, I began to shout louder while crying, "No, Bobby! Please, no!" He took me out of the church as my cries and protests got louder and louder... I was really upset, confused, angry, and did not want to let her go. I was normally a good little girl, but now I was ready to act out! I didn't know what was going to happen to my life! What was I going to do? (I kept asking myself.) My world rotated around my mother *and* I had no father!

I could only lean in and depend on my older siblings now. Bobby, knowing this, literally lifted me up and dragged me out onto the porch of St. Mark as I cried aloud and pounded on his chest with my fists just in a fit. Jonathan Avenue was straight ahead of us in view, also carrying so many bad memories about our father's tragic death. I felt like my world was falling apart, and I knew then that I would not be in Evanston for much longer. All of our idyllic time together in Evanston sadly was about to end. I saw a lot of change coming, and it was very scary for my young mind at the time.

I was in a flurry of tears when I heard a gentle voice saying, "Naomi! Naomi!" I abruptly turned away from crying and beating on Bobby's chest to see Sr. Regina and Mrs. Speaks standing there holding flowers looking at me with such compassion. Seeing them, I burst into tears more as I cried out their names in pain, not out of embarrassment of the tantrum they had just obviously witnessed, but mostly out of relief that they had made the trip to come there that day to support me in my loss. I hugged them both intently in that moment. I really felt like Ursuline Academy staff supported me throughout my ordeal, and they knew that I was hurting so bad throughout all this. For that, I am eternally grateful to Ursuline Academy of Cincinnati. They could have just sent flowers, but no, they actually showed up (and helped me a lot while Mom was sick). That has always had a lasting impression on me to be more compassionate for others, especially when they're experiencing a loss or hurting in some way. It also made me believe even more in the values of UA in that my color or poor background had nothing to do with how they felt about me *(my very first true lesson in diversity and inclusion).* They gave me hope for my future in knowing that they genuinely cared for me: the young, developing woman who deserved the same opportunities as all of their other students. That was exactly the kind of support that I needed at that time, and to this day, I am committed to returning that favor to other young women (and young men) whom I encounter that might be in the same situation. It's taught me the true value of being Christ-like.

The summer after Mom passed away I just worked like crazy. My Uncle Sherman Kinney, Jr. was a city official at the time, and he got me a summer job through the city youth employment program. I worked one floor down from him in Cincinnati's City Hall building on Plum Street. I worked a microfiche machine (something archaic now) converting city blueprints to regular sheet of paper; it was like working a huge photocopier. I also went out and did city surveys of abandoned buildings on the west side that added information to those blueprints. Those were houses along Ezzard Charles that were due for either demolition or remodeling (depending upon their condition). Even back then (the early 80s), I could see that the West End was about to change. I worked 16 hours a day: 8 hours at City Hall, then I would take a short bus trip up Gilbert Avenue to McMillan in Walnut Hills to work 8 hours at Skyline Chili. My head would slam on the pillow when I would get back home staying with my sister Cecilia (at her apartment in Avondale until I graduated).

Then I had to figure out how to get back and forth to Ursuline Academy every day for my senior year. Word got back to St. Mark, and another angel appeared in the name of Mrs. Alberta Hairston. Her cheerful daughter Susan had been accepted to Ursuline Academy as a freshman. She lived in Evanston also, and she and Susan would have to go there every day anyway. So, this "angel" volunteered to *(and did)* drive from Evanston to Avondale each morning to pick me up, and then we took the 19-mile ride out to Ursuline Academy in Blue Ash. At the end of each school day she would take me back to Ceal's apartment in Avondale. She did that my entire senior year, and I am eternally grateful to her for that. *(Note: her daughter Susan graduated UA also, but died years later due to an undisclosed illness. May she rest in heavenly peace.)*

My senior year at Ursuline Academy of Cincinnati was somber, and my few friends who knew what I was experiencing expressed their condolences in the cafeteria as our class song Bruce Springsteen's "Born to Run" played in the background on the common stereo we all debated over for control of which station we would hear. I mostly hung out with the other Black girls in my class (Robin, Tanya, Lana, Denise). My friend Tammy and I also grew closer, went on off-campus school projects together often, and hung out around Cincinnati after school sometimes (she was an award-winning diver and she trained at University of

Cincinnati down near where I lived), because Tammy had a car! She would pop in a cassette tape *(something also outdated now but I still have some!)*, and we would ride with the music blasting singing along. We often listened to the Doors ("Hello, I Love You" and "Light My Fire"), the Cars ("My Best Friend's Girl" and "Just What I Needed"), Jackson Browne ("Running on Empty"), and Neil Young ("The Needle and the Damage Done" – coincidentally, a song about suicide and "Heart of Gold"). She was a good listener to all my lamenting, sadness, and depression at the time, and it was nice to have a close UA friend with whom I could talk about my loss (something I did not always do so openly with my other UA friends). But mostly I was studying or working; I just dove into my academics and raised my GPA in preparation for graduation from Ursuline Academy, which praise God, my final year was all paid for. I also dove into learning the Spanish language, and Mrs. Ruthanne Palmer at Ursuline Academy also encouraged me to take it there all four years (another "angel" in my path). But, I could not wait to be able to escape Cincinnati for college to avoid all this pain. But preparing for my high school graduation proved difficult as I was still heavily grieving my mother's recent death.

I used my own money from working at Skyline Chili (and money I had saved working with Uncle Sherman over the past summer) to pay for all my graduation needs and to buy the pattern and material for my graduation dress which had to be white. My cousin Anthony King (top seamstress in Cincinnati, apprentice to none other than THE Alfreda

Kinney) agreed to make the dress for me for nothing (probably out of obligation to my mother for teaching him the craft). I met with him weekly leading up to my graduation for fittings, but every time we'd have to take an intermittent pause so I could just cry my eyes out, knowing I was preparing for this great event in my life for which neither of my parents would be present. He would look at me sadly patting me and say "It's going be ok, Nay"; he was so patient with me, and I thank him for being a shoulder to cry on then and for making that beautiful lace dress for me. I kept stress eating and gaining weight, so each time I would come for a fitting he would have to take out the waste a bit more. Our graduation (class of 1981) was at Rockdale Temple in the affluent Amberley Village section of Cincinnati, where Bobby proudly placed the laurel leaf on my head (as this was a tradition that fathers do for daughters at graduation, he stood in for Daddy). The armpit of my hand-made dress ripped at the graduation ceremony when I went to hug someone, but I worked through my wardrobe malfunction by tightly holding the dozen roses we each were given that day. I was relieved, and happy to have a dozen roses I had never held before in my life. My siblings continued to make me feel special, taking me out to lunch afterwards, but I remember feeling empty while they were all smiling at me. But it, again, was my dear siblings who were here trying to make this day special for me with so much love. I could not ask for more. I ended up graduating from Ursuline Academy with honors, but was also full of life's lessons at the tender age of 17.

I worked all summer at Skyline until it was time for me to go off to college. Right before I did so, Uncle George Kinney and Aunt Kathleen invited me to come to Lansing, Michigan to visit them and take some time off before I got weighed down with my studies in college. And I could use a getaway to relax and clear my mind before then. Besides, it had been a while since they had visited our house on Grantwood. They lived in Michigan in the summers, but drove around the southern US in their mobile home in the winter time to avoid the Lansing snow. They would often stop through Cincinnati on their way south when they'd do so, and we always got a visit then. So, I packed my one duffle bag, boarded a Greyhound Bus, and headed north to Lansing. I stayed there for a week, and they treated me like a princess. Aunt Kathleen asked me each night "what would you like for dinner?" No one had ever asked ME that question; I ate what was served. But I remember responding with "Beef stew maybe with some corn muffins", and it would be on the table for dinner that evening. She took me to her health spa, and it was the first time I had ever been in a jacuzzi. I remember telling her, "Ahhh, this is the life. When I get older, I'm definitely getting me a health club membership like this!" (And I did so, remembering what an escape it brought her.) Uncle George was always fixing something, having built his entire house with little assistance. He was a construction/engineering maverick, super smart and athletic. He and Aunt Kathleen were older (he is my father's oldest brother), but he was still in tip-top shape. He would ride me around Lansing on his bicycle built for two, and would tell me don't worry about paddling – making him do all the work. It was so much fun to be with them both, and I am eternally grateful for them inviting me there at this particularly tender time in my life when I so much needed that.

(If you know of any young girl dealing with a loss of her mother particularly, contact empowerHER - Youth Mentoring Program for Girls Facing Loss (empoweringher. org) *to get her the help that she needs. Encourage her to reach out to her clergy, her family, friends, a counselor, or a mental health professional. If you can, mentor her or get her a mentor that can help guide her daily steps toward her success in life. Ask her directly "What do you need?", and then follow-up on the need. There are many young ladies out there who are in the position that I was in. If you have the time and the heart, seek them out! This was critical for me to have this support, and this is why I have mentored many young women throughout my life in any way I can. We all need help getting through life's troubles occasionally, but young Black females going through this kind of trauma warrant even more support and resources.*

My direct advice to <u>any</u> young underaged woman who finds herself in a situation like mine of losing either one or both parents is to first know that it all will be ok. Be still. Pray to God. Begin reaching out to those trusted resources available to you to help you navigate the pain, the anger, the blinding grip of grief. Don't let it stagnate you. You must persevere through the pain, because there is more promise *to your life down the road... you just can't see it now in your grief. God is always with you, whether you realize that now or not. You have only one, full life to live – go out and live it to your best, and let no one steal your value or your joy! God bless you, and I'm praying for you!)*

*****

After my Mom's death, I felt like I had no real residence, since the house on Grantwood was sold. I lived between my sisters Karen and then onto Ceal's for a bit, and then I eventually ended up living with my namesake (Aunt Chick) in her small apartment on Montgomery Road right across from St. Mark church. I got really into my roller skating to relieve my stress, and disco was slowly dying, but not my love of music. I carried my 8-track tape player Karen had given me everywhere (even on my 10-speed bike) to amuse me when I got bored. I only had Chic's "Risque" ("Good Times" and "My Forbidden Lover"), George Benson's "Give Me the Night" (title cut and "Love x Love"), and Raydio and Ray Parker Jr.'s "Rock On" ("Hot Stuff" and "You Can't Change That") 8-track tapes in my possession, so I would play them over and over again (I know *all* the words to *all* these songs). When I got to the Royale Skating Rink on Gilbert to have some fun with Monica and Deneen we would hear Vaughan Mason and Crew's "Roll Bounce", "Ring My Bell" by Anita Ward", "Take Your Time" by the S.O.S. Band, and "I'm Ready" by Kano. I worked a lot at Skyline in between school during this time, trying to occupy my brain and my time with some positivity.

To help work through my grief and depression, my Ursuline Academy counselors referred me to a grief support group for teenagers; it was called T.O.U.C.H. (Teens Offering Understanding, Compassion, and Hope. I first resisted being involved with them, but now I will never forget this acronym, because they helped me to work through my sadness, feelings of helplessness, and my anger I was holding at that time as a teen. They took me on field trips and various retreats out in the country in the nearby Indiana countryside. I took my first van ride to Indiana on the first retreat late at night, I remember I felt angry that I had to have these "strangers" help me with this, lonely and isolated from my culture and from my family… I was just hoping for something, ANYTHING good to happen in my life at this point, so I was willing to try anything new that was positive. But the farm they took us to in Indiana was rustic, open, and beautiful, and I really love nature being the tomboy I was. So, when I got there, Mother Nature took over, and the ruggedness of the beautiful Indiana countryside allowed me the time to be still, get in touch with God, and have some serious conversations with Him to help me come to a better understanding of why both my parents had been taken from me so early… why He would put me in this position in life. He *must* think I'm very strong! It was strengthening and inspiring for me, very helpful and healing, soothing some of the hurt in my heart. In the evenings we prayed together, had open discussions about our feelings, and always had a good nourishing meal together. During these "excursions", I never wanted for anything really, so I never really could complain. I was grateful just to get through each day then. I now realize that God puts "angels" in our path when we least expect it, and looking back, these "strangers" played that role at the time. I returned to Cincinnati after a few trips there so renewed and refreshed with a better perspective of life, of myself, and my unique personal situation.

Elizabeth Kübler-Ross' book *"On Death and Dying" (Scribner, 1969)* was suggested reading for me then, and it did help me work through my emotional stages of grief at the time:

- **Denial** – Avoidance, Confusion, Shock, Fear

- **Anger** – Frustration, Irritation, Anxiety

- **Bargaining** – Struggling to find meaning, Reaching out to others, Telling one's story

- **Depression** – Overwhelmed, Helplessness, Hostility, Flight

- **Acceptance** – Exploring options, New plan in place, moving on

I went through all of these, but I've always tried to stay in that last one – Acceptance (of God's Will). The book also gave good advice like "Learn to get in touch with the silence within yourself and know that everything in this life has a purpose." I also learned that I am not alone; so many other young people like me were also suffering from a loss in their family. I also learned that I'm not a bad person for my loss, and that it was not my fault (I did blame myself sometimes). I was given hope (through God's grace and the love of others) that all of this was surmountable with time, counseling, and definitely leaning on my faith in God.

"If any man among you seem to be religious, and bridleth not his tongue, but deceiveth his own heart, this man's religious is vain. Pure religious and undefiled before God and the Father is this: to visit the fatherless and widows in their affliction, and to keep himself unspotted from the world."
– James 1:26-27

"Happy is he that hath the God of Jacob for his help, whose hope is in the Lord his God: which made heaven, and earth, the sea, and all that is therein is: which keepeth truth forever: which executeth judgement for the oppressed: which giveth food to the hungry. The Lord looseth the prisoners. The Lord openeth the eyes of the blind: The Lord raiseth them that are bowed down; the Lord loveth the righteous. The Lord preserveth the strangers; he relieveth the fatherless and widow; but the way of the wicked he turneth upside down. The Lord shall reign forever, even thy God, O Zion, unto all generations. Praise ye the Lord." **– Psalms 146:5-10**

Chapter 11:
A Light at the End of the Tunnel

*"Remembering mine affliction and my misery, the wormwood and the gall, my soul hath them still in remembrance, and is humbled in me. This I recall to my mind; therefore, I have hope. It is of the Lord's mercy that we are not consumed, because his compassions fail not. They are new every morning: great is thy faithfulness. The Lord is my portion, sayeth my soul; therefore, I will hope in Him. The Lord is good to those that wait for Him, to the soul that seeketh Him." – **Lamentations 3: 19-25**

I received two academic scholarships as I graduated with honors from Ursuline Academy, and with the influence of my former St. Mark math teacher and mentor Mrs. Brenda Madison (another "angel" in my life), I decided to attend nearby Central State University (CSU – her alma mater) in Wilberforce, Ohio. I was living with Aunt Chick at the time; she and Mrs. Madison coordinated closely to make sure I had everything I needed to transition into college life. Mrs. Madison, an alum and strong proponent of Central State University (an HBCU – Historical Black Colleges & Universities) in Wilberforce, Ohio, recruited me to go there telling me "Nay, we getting' ready to get you another scholarship! You ARE going to college, girl!" I couldn't see it at the time still going through my cycles of grief and just in shock at being parentless. Now, I was even more scared if anyone were to ask about my parents even more than when I was at Ursuline. Before I got accepted to CSU, she drove me there for a quick tour of the campus. When I arrived on that campus and began walking around seeing all the Black folks, I felt like I was right back in Evanston in Cincinnati! And after attending an all-girl predominantly white Catholic high school, my eyes were redirected toward all the handsome young *Black men* walking the campus from cities across the region and from across America, trying to get their education too. Attending school with the opposite sex was something I had never experienced before as a young woman, so it was exciting to be in that environment for many reasons. Here the students were not always their best when they arrived, but with mentoring, guidance, and opportunity like I received would eventually get a college education and go on to do greater things across this country (with the help of these "angels"). Each student at an HBCU has a story about how someone got them there – that was surely the case with me and Central State University in Wilberforce, Ohio.

I felt comfortable on the campus, and with "Mrs. Mad" there guiding me around this felt right. (I trusted her judgement, I knew she cared about me, she taught me math so well at St. Mark that would eventually come in handy, and she also knew my Mom from working at St. Mark with her. I ended up being her baby sitter to kids "Jay" and "Bilenda", especially every New Year's Eve.) So, I followed Mrs. Mad's guidance that day in a leap of faith and love (she and her husband "Uncle Bill" have always been great support). We eventually ended up in Art Thomas' office (Office of the University President) that afternoon still touring the campus, and I then found out that they were classmates at CSU! She quickly introduced me, "I need for you to meet an amazing potential CSU student, and her name is Naomi Kinney!" We all three sat down and talked, Mrs. Madison explained my situation of having no parents (and just recently losing one) to him, and then she made a final demand of him (not a request!). In her directive and commanding voice, she *told* him (index finger pointing), "Art, you need to accept this girl to CSU *and* give her a scholarship considering her grades! She needs CSU, and CSU needs her! You all could use an excellent student like Naomi!" I could not have had a better cheerleader that day. The next thing I knew, I received word that I would be receiving my *third* scholarship from the university in order to attend there! I had applied and been accepted to Old Dominion University (in VA since my brothers were in Norfolk in the Navy at the time), and I also got wooed by Middlebury Language School while I was at Ursuline Academy (in VT but could not stand the thought of being that far from my family). But this locked it in for my future at Central State. I had never heard of Wilberforce, Ohio in my Ohio history lessons in school, but I would eventually find out how historic this place was/is, allowing me to learn more about my state's history, my personal heritage, and my country.

"Mrs. Mad" (as we so affectionately called her) helped me apply for an Ohio Pell grant, and with my scholarships, I was headed to Central State University for college (something that I did not think was possible a year earlier going through my grief). Aunt Chick drove me to campus in Wilberforce in her big black sedan on registration day, but I ran into a few roadblocks. While getting all matters settled in the financial aid office, the lady at the counter told me "We need proof of your parents' death on file before we can apply your Pell grant money. We need a copy of their death certificates." I pleaded to the lady and started crying, already still grieving, dumbfounded that she did not believe me when I told her both my parents are deceased. They probably have heard that story before from other students (for whom that was *not* the case). So, I left the long line crying aloud in front of all the other students looking on, and one of my close college buddies (Larry Lyles also class of 1985) still remembers witnessing that happening to me that day, as he was in the registration line also. I felt defeated, but when I went back to Aunt Chick who was patiently waiting for me in the car to make sure I got on campus ok, we had to figure out our next steps. I could get my pass from Housing to move into the dorms, so "Auntie" told me "move your stuff into the dorm, come back to the car, and we'll go to Cincinnati to get the death certificates. So, I had to drive home with Aunt Chick, spend the night, go to the Bureau of Vital Statistics on Elm Street in Cincinnati, pay the fee to get two death certificates (my father's and my mother's), and then Aunt Chick took me back to CSU the next day, dropped me off at my dorm room and kept rolling back to Cincinnati. I eventually got registered (all death certificates on file now and Pell grant money released to the school), and with my scholarships my whole year's tuition was paid (I even got refunded money at the end of every year, which I never complained about).

I arrived on the campus of Central State University depressed and still heavily grieving the loss of my dear mother, my only parent. However, I was determined to make good on the three academic scholarships I had earned and to prove I was worthy of the support of all the people who had pulled for me to get there. But it meant that I definitely had to graduate within four years, the time limit on my scholarships. I was surely determined to make that happen, and I didn't know it then, but I would also get a lot of support at CSU to make that happen. In my freshman year, I moved into Williamson Hall on the campus on the fourth floor, so I got lots of exercise. Like at Ursuline Academy of Cincinnati, I kept to myself and focused on my studies to avoid getting any questions about what I was going through. My first roommate was Paula Randolph with whom I had my First Holy Communion at St. Mark *(and I would later run into other St. Mark kids on campus like Angela Powell)*. Then two days after arriving and moving in two doors down was a smiling, warm and friendly girl from Detroit, Michigan named Sabrina Coleman. We ended up being very good friends there (and beyond), as she always wanted to tag along with me at the library when she could (I was there constantly, my favorite quiet place to study on campus). The second half of my Freshman year, I moved into Hunter Hall (next door to Williamson) and in with roommate Jeralyn Jackson from Bellfontaine, Ohio (the city in Ohio with the highest altitude at Campbell Hill). She and I also became very good friends at CSU (and beyond). I first was a Communications major (a DJ, for my love of music), but in my sophomore years I got more serious about my studies and changed my major to a double major of English Literature and Foreign Languages (Spanish), since I continued studying the language at CSU with Dr. William Felker in their Foreign Language Department. Dr. Terence Glass was also a great guide for me as head of the English Department. The summers in between studying at CSU, I worked at a summer camp in Harrison, Ohio (on the Indiana/Ohio line) called Fort Scott Camps. The first summer I was a cabin counselor, and the next summer I got another job there as Director of Nature. I was a lifeguard (Red Cross certified), I rode horses twice a week, and led the girl campers on long hikes through trails and on canoe trips down the Little Miami river which flowed nearby, returning bronzed and hair blonde on the edges from so much sun exposure (looking a lot like Mom when she returned from her trips to Lansing, Michigan to visit Uncle George and Aunt Kathleen, and when I went there also). During this time, I was in the best physical shape of my life, being so active. Knowing the benefits of taking advantage of every ideal opportunity that comes your way in life, I prayed to God that more great opportunities would come my way and promised not to squander any. When the summers were over, I would go for a brief stay with my sister Cecilia (who had a growing family during this time, but I was just grateful to have a place to lay my head), and then I would get right back to campus and to my studies at CSU.

While at CSU in my junior year, Dr. Felker announced the opportunity for three foreign language students to go to study in Mexico. What was the requirement to get to go? – Write a paper about why you feel you deserve to go study in Mexico. Well, boy did I write a paper! I explained how I had been studying the Spanish language for 8 years, how I tested into Spanish IV in my freshman year, and how I was a tutor of the language for the other students. In 1984, I won one of the three scholarships to study and travel in Mexico (the other two went to other deserving students), and I lived with the host family of Señora Maria Gomez Palafox for six months, the experience of a lifetime. Our group of American students received orientation in Guadalajara, Jalisco for a week, and then we all went onto Morelia, Michoacán to attend the CECEMMAC school there. I could write a book alone about all the things that occurred in that small span of time in my life, but I was able to see the world beyond Cincinnati, Ohio like I had never seen it before in my life. That one trip opened up my world perspective on people, culture, and the Spanish language. After this amazing experience, I came back from Mexico speaking Spanish fluently "with a heavy Mexican accent" per Dr. Felker. It was time to return to CSU to the Breezeway parties, May weekend fun, and bologna sandwiches, K colas, and Little Debbie treats as late-night snacks... my senior year in college! At this point, I was very excited about what life had to offer me. This was also a time when MTV was white-hot in popularity, and they showed all the videos of the most popular musical artists of the time like Michael Jackson's "Thriller", Prince's "Purple Rain", Boy George's "Karma Chameleon", and "True" by Spandau Ballet. When I was back on the CSU campus, I was going now happy to go to the dances and parties (like I had never done before in high school), chanting "O-H-I-O" like the Ohio Players did it in their song. We also listened to many other great bands that came out of Ohio like Heat Wave, Slave, or the Isley Brothers. Some of the dorm rooms also had Trouble Funk's "Drop the Bomb" blasting, which is where I got my first taste of DC native "go-go" music. I had gotten a taste of it on at the roller-skating rink in Cincinnati with Chuck Brown's "Bustin' Loose", which they played at the Royale skating rink there. But I had no idea how much *more* go-go music I would soon be hearing quite frequently very soon.

I graduated from Central State University with a 3.48 (very close to magna cum laude) in 1985, and felt so relieved that I had achieved this feat with no parental support. But I had no one there to celebrate with me at graduation. Yet I was still determined to get up there, put on my cap and gown, and accept that degree even if it was all by myself. So, leading up to graduation day, I was a little depressed sitting in my dorm room waiting, but was still determined. I was just so happy that my college graduation day was coming soon. On graduation day, as President Art Thomas called off each student's name, he shook his or her hand as they crossed the stage to accept their degree. When my turn came and they announced "Naomi Joan Kinney, magna cum laude" I heard a roar from the upper bleachers, and looked up to see Ceal, Bobby, Carl, Karen with their kids (and I don't remember who else), but it was a big crowd back there cheering ME on! Here, I thought no one would bother to make that 90-minute drive up to the campus from Cincinnati to Wilberforce to see me graduate; I thought they forgot when I sent them their invitations. They ALL showed up! I went back to my seat clutching my new degree and feeling so relieved, elated, and loved all at the same time. After graduation, I met my family outside the gym and hugged them all so excitedly. My siblings did it again!

My experiences in my college years at Central State University were the best in my lifetime; I learned so much and always felt at home on that campus (it was my home for four years!). At that time, I had few bills, a full ride on tuition, few responsibilities, and I had great opportunities. I only had to worry about studying and staying out of trouble, and that was something at which I was already well disciplined. So, college at CSU was a *lot* of fun for me and taught me a lot about my heritage, about Ohio, and about what my future possibilities could be. It is the *personal* guidance and mentoring that many Black students receive at HBCUs from the teachers there along with the genuine friendships that I forged with the other students there that means so much to me to this day. We bonded there while on that campus studying, learning, growing, and experiencing some hunger (in many ways) together. But we definitely had some fun! I am grateful that my path in life took me through Wilberforce, Ohio. Once I was graduated later that afternoon, my siblings helped me pack my few things remaining from my dorm room, and Karen drove me and all my college junk back to Ceal's place on Woodburn until I made my next move with the help of another dear sibling. My sibs have always been "tag-teaming" for me, and I am every grateful. Although so many tragic events had occurred in my short past and at the dawn of my life, I became to realize in my heart and mind that God did indeed have special plans for me all along. He was/is simply using me for His purpose... soon to be my life's mission.

Chapter 12:
A Whole New World

"You're not from around here, are you?" is the question I received when I arrived in Washington, DC after my graduation from Central State University. I moved away from Ohio to live there following my big sister Angela who had just graduated from Georgetown (also studying Foreign Languages). They really got confused when I would start speaking Spanish too, and with my appearance, could not tell whether I was Hispanic or not. I felt like I could use my ability to speak Spanish more in DC, which is why I asked Angie if I could come and be with her after school. "Yeah, but you gotta get work as soon as possible when you get here. But if you can type, you can get a job easily in DC", she assured me. I had some money saved, was ready to get to work after school (after relaxing for a couple of weeks), and was confident in me being a hard worker that I could find something there soon. I realized then in the late 80s that the Hispanic population in DC was exploding (particularly those from El Salvador and other Central American countries due to the civil unrest there). DC would be needing more bilingual people like my sister and I to help communities communicate across cultures. So, yes, God puts you where you need to be.

Angie picked me up at the Greyhound Bus station on New York Avenue in busy NW DC (you must specify which quadrant of the city you're in, I learned, or you're gonna be a lost soul there). Although already exhausted, and Angie without a car, she warned me about all the precautions to take while living in "the big city" as we walked 8 blocks with all my belongings to her small studio apartment on 3rd and G Streets, N.W. DC near Chinatown. (So, we always had good Chinese food just a walk away, but it was also a draw for a lot of homeless people of which there were many in DC then – ironically, this area of DC has condos and high-rise apartments on the same corner now, is now a highly gentrified area of the District). I became exhausted, but my adrenaline was racing, excited about where to start and so grateful about my future in this new "big city". It was good that we did not have cars, because it kept us in shape, and we could see the city in ways cars can't. There were/are bike racks everywhere to secure our bikes, and you could even take your bike on the Metro (the subway train which was also interesting to learn about DC). We rode our bikes everywhere (as did many others in DC, not something I saw too much of in Ohio), and often to the National Mall which was just blocks away. We literally lived in the center of the city.

One Sunday we had a picnic of sorts, gathering some snacks, drinks, our frisbee, and a blanket to lay out on "the Mall" after church and walked there leaving our bikes behind. Being new to DC and away from Ohio in this fast-moving city was exciting, and I was just finding a way to blend in with the help of my ever-protective big sister. It was a beautiful day, and we carried our little radio with us listening to songs like Whitney Houston's "You Give Good Love", Loose Ends "Hangin' on a String", Sade's "Sweetest Taboo", Isley-Jasper-Isley's "Caravan of Love", Lisa Lisa & Cult Jam's "Can You Feel the Beat?", and Prince's "Raspberry Beret", throwing our frisbee back and forth. Sometimes we would ride as far as Arlington Cemetery in VA. On this Sunday we walked on foot to our apartment from the National Mall, and we were well sated from our snacks, full of sisterly fun for the day and still chatting it up (I think Angie was really enjoying having a family member in town with her after being solo in DC for a while), and we were ready to get home and rest for our jobs the next day (Angie worked at the gift shop at the U.S. Library of Congress, and I had nabbed a temporary job as a receptionist). As we walked home it was quiet on the downtown DC streets, quieter than the normal weekday. As the music played we sang along, but when the commercials came on the radio, we eventually noticed and heard other steps behind us. Looking back from a distance, there was a guy in a black cape, black shirt and top, and black wide brim hat walking behind us at the same page. With minimal people on the street, it was obvious that we has following us, and Angie took notice of it first, grabbing me by the back of my elbow, pushing me forward saying "pick up the pace, Nay... that weirdo behind us in black is following us." I peeked back, and it seemed like she was right, so then I definitely put some pep in my step. When I looked back, he also picked up his pace to keep up with us!

Now, we were both tripping out. I was feeling like "Pollyanna" being from Ohio, because I had never had anything confrontational with a stranger like this happen to me there! I was terrified once Angie told me calmly, "When we get to the corner, run like hell to the apartment entrance so he won't be able to see where we live!" And on the count of three, we both took off running toward our apartment building's entrance as soon as we turned that corner. We rushed upstairs to our second-floor apartment which looked out over onto the front of the building; rushing over to the front window, we could see the guy in the black cape and wide brim hat run past the front of the building, his black cape flapping in the wind behind him. We sat there and prayed and hugged each other for a minute until we calmed down from our scary escapade. Ever since, we tried to ride our bikes as often as we could to make sure we could always have a speedier getaway if needed. In the DC streets at the time (mid 80s) there was a lot of crime, homelessness, drugs, and prostitution. It was hard to avoid, but "Ang" and I were blessed to always maintain our professional presence, blowing past all this negativity around us in the city.

We eventually both got really good jobs, and moved into a nice renovated basement apartment near Logan Circle in

N.W. DC. I remember as Angie and I moved from our old studio apartment into the new luxury apartment building there, we were singing the theme from the Jefferson's "And We're Movin' on Up!" It was an area of DC with high prostitution at the time, so the evenings and weekends got quite interesting (now another totally gentrified neighborhood in DC). I was here for not quite six months when I got a call from my college buddy Sabrina Coleman, asking if she could come to DC, because "not much was happening on the job front in Detroit", as "Bree" put it. I could use a familiar friend with me in DC, but really had not established myself just yet, so I had to ask Angie. Like when I arrived, Angie said "Yes, but she's gotta get a job to help us pay to live here!" And just like that, I had a Central State friend here on the east coast to hang out with, and go clubbing at the many DC party spots, and to hang out there. I eventually would be a lot of other Central State University alumni living in the "DMV" (DC, Maryland, and Virginia Metro area).

When I arrived in DC I had a bit of a culture shock. You could/can stand on the street corner in DC, and within 10 minutes you can hear three or four different languages being spoken (sometimes more). This, I noticed, was a very different social environment than what I grew up in also. It was so much more multicultural, multilingual, and diverse, and I loved it! Many people looked very different and unique like Angie and I, and that was/is totally ok, accepted, and even welcomed here... the more diverse and unique you are, the better. And I was just young enough with some money in my pocket (for the first time in my life), full of energy and promise, and feeling such independence and freedom from my academics. Life was beginning to look up a bit as I got into my profession of training and development. I felt like I was on top of the world every time I looked at the Capitol Building living it up in DC with my big sister going to elaborate parties, and seeing THE big 4th of July fireworks on the national mall every year. I often had to pinch myself as I looked at the national monuments or the DC skyline (beautiful as you drive in from VA on I-395 north) thinking "this is such a great existence, Naomi. You've done pretty well in life to be living and thriving here."

My temp job landed me at a major Fortune 500 secondary mortgage banking organization. I went from Accounting Technician to Senior Training Analyst in 10 years, and worked alongside some amazing professionals (and I was proud that many of them were African-American, great role models for me). I attended some of the most awesome black-tie, elegant celebrations and cocktail parties for the first time in my life, and the most incredible annual company picnics I'll ever experience. Angie would join me at many of these events, and I would join her at her work events and after hours too. She eventually became a senior executive in the federal government, and liked her life on Capitol Hill in DC (but she began to experience some health challenges during this time). I gradually transitioned into the world of training and development in the early 90s. I received my first training on "instructional design" during this time when the training industry was just beginning to flourish. I also became a homeowner at 27 years old, and I traveled close to 40 of the 50 states training banks and S&Ls on mortgage loan reporting practices (systems training). I learned a lot about mortgage banking and also about the need for community service volunteer help across the DC community (especially regarding housing issues). I volunteered to serve for five years on the Board of Directors for a homeless shelter called Hannah House in NW DC, and I was the lead coordinator for the annual cookout that my job offered each year to the women of the shelter. I loved the thought of giving back to my community (we were raised to do so, having been recipients of this for years growing up in Ohio). So, I participated with excitement at work, winning awards for job performance (Premium Performer and All-Star Team awards) as well as winning awards for community work (Food and Friends' Crest of the WAVE Award and Inroads of Greater Washington's Outstanding Service Award). My employer got wind of my Spanish language fluency, and then my company began sending me to various conferences in partnership with Hispanic agencies (e.g., then the National Council of La Raza – NCLR, now called "UnidosUS" which is an advocacy agency, kind of like the Hispanic NAACP). During this time Diversity & Inclusion was becoming part of the required curriculum for all employees everywhere I worked (me teaching/facilitating it directly), and I would eventually find out what an important subject this would become in my role as a workplace learning professional, also impacting my mission in life.

When I turned 30 years old in DC, I had a BIG all-girl party to celebrate at my home in North Michigan Park in DC. Having family and my closest friends was a great memory for my time there. On the professional front, I eventually took on several leadership positions in training and development at various major organizations and some federal agencies, but then transitioned into the healthcare industry with my language ability. In 1997, I accepted the position of Director of Hospital Education at Providence Hospital DC, working there for eight years. It was the most gratifying job that I've ever had in my life, being under the best boss ever (Mr. Paul Wellington Smith, along working with many great colleagues, all of us whom still stay in touch to this day). While working alongside the Daughters of Charity nuns, I learned so much about their important spiritual mission of serving the poor and those in need. I led the monthly trips that would take hospital staff to Emmitsburg, MD to see the shrine of Elizabeth Ann Seton (founder of Daughters of Charity and visited the replica of the Grotto of Lourdes, originally in France) for greater understanding of that mission. As a regulatory mandate, I created the Interpreter Services Program at this Catholic hospital (accommodating 5 main languages, 12 human interpreters to schedule, and a 24/7 telephonic service), something I'm very proud of, having studied the Spanish language for many years and studied abroad in Mexico. And I also became a certified Healthcare Interpreter in the process along with several other hospital employees that I encouraged to do so. It allowed me to meet and get to know other employees of the hospital from other areas of the globe who spoke other languages (Spanish, French, Amharic, Hindi, and Mandarin Chinese specifically were the languages we included in the telephonic and in-person interpreter services at the hospital). Leading this effort was absolutely fantastic – a language-lover's dream come true!

I was a young Black female professional in DC, wore business suits all the time at work (but flashed my attractiveness in cute outfits after hours when I could), worked for top organizations, traveled independently across the US for work and for pleasure, won many awards, saw the many interesting sites in DC on the weekends with my sister and friends, and was using my language abilities... life could not get any better than this! But lo and behold in 1990, I became a member of the greatest Black Greek sorority on the planet *(in my biased opinion, of course):* Delta Sigma Theta Sorority, Inc. and in THE Federal City Alumnae Chapter (DC). I became part of an amazing and powerful group of Christian college-educated women *(predominantly African-American)* who wanted to do the same thing I did: serve my community and my God. I wanted to commit to being around such great, accomplished, and positive Black female role models. I receive so much physical, mental, spiritual, motivational love and support from my "sorors" *(they just don't know).* They all were a true blessing from God and an inspiration to help keep me going, considering all the challenges I have had to navigate as a young black woman. For this, I am committed to always reciprocating this to all of my "little sistas" out there that are in my path, hoping to be their "angel" as well to help them along their paths in life. Me and my sorors do this amazing kind of inspiring work *together* now to enhance the local DC community and our world. Being a Delta is something that I have wanted to do since college, because Mrs. Brenda Madison, my mentor and guide at a critical time in my life spoke frequently about her amazing Delta sorors, and many of them helped me get through college. I thought to myself "If they're anything like her, I want to be around those kind of women – I feel safe there." So, yes, God puts you where you need to be (serving his people and finding your mission in life). At this time, I also was recruited by one of my Fannie Mae co-workers (Janet Rivera Tucker, also a Latina who encouraged me with my Spanish-speaking) to be part of an awesome mentor pro-gram (Futures 500) that matched me with other young minority women who attended H.D. Woodson High School in DC to form great relationships *(mentoring - a topic for another book within itself because some amazing part-nerships have blossomed here too in my life)*. Then I con-nected with my mentee, good friend, and Godmother to my daughter, LaShone Earl Wilson (who I mentioned at the beginning of this book). We have been connected since the 90s, and now she inspires me teaching me about yoga and meditation to keep my life balanced.

Since I had no kids in the 90s and still had the burning need to do some work in radio and television, I would often volunteer to work in the studio at WPFW/Pacifica Radio 89.3 FM in the Adams Morgan section of Northwest DC, a community radio funded by its listeners. Dedicated to jazz, justice, and the community, they have a wide variety of shows from talk, to music (jazz to go-go, to R&B, to revolutionary music), to listener fundraising drives, and I was always working the phones and ended up on the air to encourage the many local listeners to call in to donate and to keep WPFW the DC classic tradition it is. I later took a 6-month course with the Columbia School of Broadcasting, and received an official license with the Federal Communications Commission (FCC) to be an on-air broadcaster. Subsequently, I started doing some production and camera work with DC's Public Access TV, and created two videos that (while using the station's equipment) they kept and would put on the air intermittently. The two videos were: For "DC on the Move". I lugged the camera equipment down to SW DC's West Potomac Park out on the peninsula to a place in the park called Haines Point. I filmed airplanes taking off, boats racing by on the Potomac, and cars/bikers/skaters racing thru the park; then I went back to the station and edited the video with the production staff, adding in Lenny Kravitz' (the love of my life!) "Fly Away" to the sound track. It was pretty cool. The second video was simply a beginner's "Spanish 101" language class in the studio with a chalk board and a few props. DC Public Access TV added both to their "back-up programs" line-up, so they both got a bit of air time. Pretty soon, as I would turn the corner while walking in the hospital, I would have someone stop me and ask, "Hey, were you on DC TV?" My response would be "Yes!" with a smile. "Did you see me teaching Spanish?" I used a lot of these skills learned in broadcasting to do some voice-over work on training videos. I still have my voice-over demo MP3 where my voice is featured in several commercial clips in English and in Spanish. Attaining that MP# demo was a dream come true. And when I met Donnie Simpson at BET during a filming of Video Soul at the BET studios in Northeast DC, I thought I would die! He autographed a picture for me that said "From green eyes to green eyes!"

In the mid-90s, I was still obsessed with music, recording a lot on CDs (though I still have some cassettes with Brian McKnight, Mary J. Blige, and Najee, as I started to get into smooth jazz during this time), and I shared cassette tapes and CDs with my friends (some of them still probably have some too, I hope still enjoying the music). I was mega-hyped and proud when homegirl and St. Mark First Holy Communion class-mate Penny Ford could be heard singing "I got the power!" on "The Power – Snap!) song in the DC clubs at this time. I was enjoying the sounds of a lot of other "New Jack" artists like Next, Jagged Edge, SWV, Boyz II Men, Toni Tone Tony, Jade, Monica, Brandy, Aliyyah, Usher Raymond, Genuine, etc. on the many R&B radio stations of DC then, while also attending outdoor and indoor concerts featuring R&B but also jazz artists like Michael Franks, David Sanborn, Gerald Albright, and Stanley Turrentine. Although my musical taste was smoothing out, I still liked a good New York mix tape every now and then that would include some LL Cool J, EPMD, Busta Rhymes, KRS1, Method Man, MC Lyte, and Queen Latifah. As a single homeowner, I would have some great cookouts and card parties that came with all this great music too, so life in the 90s was cool and exciting learning so much about so many different people in this truly diverse city.

While working at Providence Hospital, I was also learning a lot about people and humanity in my every-day experiences. We also experienced the turn of the century there. I spent the night working at the hospital (which was only three blocks from my house so not really an inconvenience), but it turned out to be more of a whimper than a bang. The thing I am most proud of in this world is giving birth to my daughter Julia while working at Providence Hospital, and want to thank everyone at the hospital for helping me bring her into the world safely, which happened to have been in the fall of 2001 during the time of September 11th, the Anthrax scare, and the Sniper Attacks that terrorized DC. "Auntie Mimi" (my mentor Brenda Madison) even made a dedicated trip from Cincinnati to help me in my first days with my child, continually telling me out loud "Naomi, you are my child!" I already knew she was one of my "angels", but this God-send came to me *again* at another critical point in my life. She and my entire "village" helped me move into motherhood and back to my Directorship at the hospital just blocks away. Working at Providence Hospital allowed me to practice my faith actively each day. I could go to the chapel in the hospital whenever I wanted to and did so often. My job kept me financed to maintain my home and lifestyle. It also kept me healthy with all the great health-related information I was exposed to daily, it allowed me to do direct community outreach (to *all* ethnic groups and people from all walks of life), and I also had the opportunity to provide interpreter services (and translations) with the Hispanic community... continually fulfilling my life's mission and God's plan for me. He would put many situations before me where I would have the opportunity to do His work...

One day at the hospital, I had an interesting encounter with a nice Latino man that was another "epiphany" of sorts about where God has placed me (and why I know it's *always* for a reason). This older man (but not elderly) entered the lobby of Providence Hospital on this sunny afternoon, and I happened to be there at the front desk, probably completing an interpreter services assignment or after delivering a session of mandatory safety training to hospital staff. It was late in the work day and almost time to go home (and this was before I had my daughter so I had no real need to rush home). As Director of the Hospital Education department, I would teach all hospital staff to not only know hospital safety and patient/visitor protocols, but also to *anticipate* the needs of anyone coming in the door – look for the signs of need and provide everyone with equal concern and quality customer service and patient care. The man was looking all around at the signs like he was in a strange place, and he definitely looked like a candidate for a self-introduction. I approached him slowly smiling, and said "Hi, sir, I'm Naomi... Can I help you find your way?", a question I would often teach the staff to use to open a conversation with patients, guests, and visitors of the hospital to politely offer assistance. He looked at me and nodded, but pointed to his mouth and shook his head stating in broken English "I no speak 'e...." I immediately broke into speaking Spanish stating, "¡Oh, está bien, señor... Puedo hablar español! ¿En qué puedo servirle Usted?" *(Oh, it's ok, sir... I can speak Spanish. How can I help you, sir?)* He went on to explain to me in Spanish that he needed to get a urinalysis test done in the lab at the hospital to get cleared for work. "Oh, sígueme por favor" (follow me), I told him. Knowing the process of visitors just receiving diagnostic tests at the hospital, I took him over to Admissions (his first stop to give insurance information). It being the end of the work day and some employees had left, it was rather quiet. The receptionist asked me to escort him to the Outpatient Diagnostic Clinic on the second floor. "They send 'after-hours' patients there directly', she told me. So, I tried to give him directions, but he looked at me and asked me in Spanish to show him where to go. I looked at my watch, and knowing I was not really in a rush to get home, I said "ok". We took the elevator up to the next floor, and during the ride I found out that he was from El Salvador and was here in DC trying to get work for him and his family. We got to the Outpatient Clinic's front counter and they asked me to stay to help communicate with him to fill out his paper work. "We don't have any bilingual staff on duty now." I said no problem, and always considered it a gift to help anyone with my use of the language, but it was getting later and later and I was getting a bit anxious and impatient. I thought that I could leave him there, and that *they* would escort him to the laboratory to give his urine sample (located on another floor of the hospital), but they asked *me* to escort him there.

To avoid looking annoyed to the man, I bided my patience and said "OK", and led him to the third-floor laboratory where I knew many of the staff from coming to my mandatory training sessions. When I arrived, they asked me to tell him how to urinate in the cup, how to seal the cup, how to document his name on the cup, and what would happen afterwards. They also asked me to wait for him in case something went wrong in the process. I gave him his instructions in Spanish with ease, he nodded, and went back to the private area to take care of business. When he came out, and the test was over, as we headed back to the elevator, I asked him "¿Vino Usted aquí en pie o en el autobus?" *(Did you come here on foot or on the bus?)* He said "autobus" nodding in the direction of the bus stop. I waved at him to follow me to the bus stop which was on the back of the hospital near the Emergency Room; it would literally pull into the hospital parking lot and pick up patients to take them to the nearby Brookland Station Metro (subway). When we got to the bus stop I told him, "Pues, adiós, mi amigo. ¡Qué tenga un buen día!" *(Well, goodbye, my friend. Have a good day!)* At that moment this man made a precious gesture that I will never forget in my life: He dug in his pocket and pulled out all of the crumpled-up dollars he had available there, and his hand loaded with dollars and coins, he extended his arm as if he were giving it all to me for what I had just done for him. This man actually put a monetary value on what I had just done, but I saw it as nothing and taking up my time at the end of my busy work day! I then realized that this WAS my work for the day! God placed me right in this man's path, and I did not even realize the valuable gift (of communicating across cultures) I had/have right within me. Shaking my head, I told him "No, no, señor... no puedo recibir pagos por esto - es un regalo de Dios." *(No, sir... I can't receive payment for this – it is a gift from God!)* He smiled, nodded, put his money back in his pocket saying "¡Gracias - Dios te ben-diga!" *(Thank you - God bless you!),* gave me a wave, and went through the double electronic doors to the outside of the hospital where the bus stop was. As I walked back across the hospital campus my heart was heavy. When I arrived back at my large office with a dozen large win-dows that provided a beautiful overlook of the front of the hospital I cried out of shame. Here I had SO much (God had blessed me so), and this man needed my help (and yet I was reluctant at first out of haste just to get through my day). Like him, in the past I needed many things that I had to hope to get through other thankfully kind-hearted people (I needed this especially in my youth), and I'm so glad that my "angels" did not turn me away at that time. I learned early on to be an "angel" to others, but only now did I realize that I must use this unique gift from God to do his work: LOVE my fellow man (or woman) regardless of their background, their language, their religion, their walk of life, knowing that God has placed me there in their path.

Since I first arrived in DC, I had always been tutoring Spanish privately on the side of my regular work (for whomever asked), and I would even teach English and Spanish to children in homeless shelters sometimes through my church (Cathedral of St. Matthew the Apostle on Rhode Island Avenue, N.W. DC). Now I would not only teach Spanish to hospital staff (to help them provide better patient/guest experiences and become more "culturally competent"), but as the hospital's curriculum designer, I also had the opportunity to add courses on Cultural Diversity & Inclusion to our monthly curriculum of course offerings to help employees work together better and to allow them to fearlessly and compassionately care for each and every patient equally regardless of their background, faith, ethnicity, etc. Both (language training and cultural competency training) became mandatory requirements for hospitals by their regulatory accreditation agency named the Joint Commission for Accreditation of Healthcare Organizations (JCAHO – some called "Jayco" – who performed hospital surveys every three years at that time). The nursing staff ate it up being care-givers of patients and residents (of the nursing home) from around the world, and many of them being from other countries themselves really appreciated the dialogue about revisiting our own biases, respecting others who are different than ourselves, and trying to learn from and communicate with each other more. They started inviting me onto the various nursing units to directly train the staff on how to encounter various cultures of people, accommodating their unique nuances and cultural needs.

I knew a lot about those nuances of Hispanics (e.g., the Mexican people where I studied), but I had to learn about diversity within the Hispanic community, as well as information about other races, cultures, religions, lifestyles, etc. And so, I set out to do my research to learn more about the Asian, African, Native American, and Middle eastern communities specifically. Living in DC, besides learning a LOT more about the Black community and more and more about DCs legendary "go-go" music culture, I also learned a whole lot about the LGBTQ (Lesbian, Gay, Bisexual, Transgender, Queer) community – in a city that, as of 2016, had the largest gay population. At that time Angie had lots of gay friends that she worked with her in the federal government, and one particularly good friend "Ted" died of AIDS years earlier in the mid-80s when there was a lot of fear of AIDS (right at the time I arrived in DC after college). I liken their treatment to how lepers were treated in the Bible; no one wanted to be near them. And I struggled with this at first, being raised Catholic, but I eventually realized that every human being is a Child of God and deserves love. I knew to, instead, be kind and compassionate (Christ-like) to *every* person I met because of this experience with Ted. Angie and I visited "Ted" regularly in the hospital, and it surely took an act of compassion to do so with so many fears swirling around this community. We had our years where we laughed and partied with "Ted" in his prime, but now we just prayed with him in his last hours. It was still such a blessing to have been "angels" to him as he went onto Glory.

As I reminisce on my experiences in DC in the 80s and 90s, they remind me to continue to help my fellow-man (or woman) just like many had helped us get through our rough times on Grantwood. This is my best way to give thanks to all who have helped us along our rocky way. It also taught me to think globally, realizing that our issues and conflicts are not just black and white; there are so many shades of gray within *all* our human issues, within *all* of our communities. Not to be overwhelmed, but I also realized that there are many people out there who need my particular skills and experience, and I just *have to* respond where I am physically and mentally able to do so. Now, to ask God for further guidance on how I should fit in...

At this point in my career (for twenty years in D.C.), I had been doing corporate training as a certified trainer, designing training courses and making presentations to help others personally or professionally improve at various major organizations and for some federal agencies in the DC area. I was always demonstrating my love for the Spanish language as a private tutor for various tutoring agencies and individuals around the DC area. Either in the workplace or in my community service, I have always been about trying to help people to communicate more and better among one another, committed to "bridging the gap" of communications (which is why I eventually became a certified healthcare interpreter), and doing whatever I can to help people in need. My message has always also been one of appreciating differences in culture, gender, race, religion, sexuality, etc. *"Why can't we all just get along?" as Rodney King asked in 1992, and the answer is "yes we can – if we put a little love and faith in our hearts."*

Now, I can easily say that *I have trained thousands of people* (praise God to even say that in my lifetime). But of all the many subjects I have had to deliver in my trainings, I eventually realized what a key role that Cultural Diversity & Inclusion Training would play in the workplace and in my training career. American businesses, churches, the education field, the legal arena, etc. all started noticing the importance of culture and language when handling human resources which is why I never had problems finding a job. I was always busy trying to train people "how to get along". Having studied another language, having lived abroad immersed in another culture enough to appreciate it and my own more, and having learned how to design learning (create curricula via instructional design), my work in the world of training became even more critical regarding the subject matter of Cultural Diversity & Inclusion. What would I include in this training, how to structure it, and how would my audiences respond to and/or benefit?

After all the parties at posh locations in DC, after eating at the best restaurants (like the Sequoia on DC Waterfront and Inn at Little Washington in VA – superb!), after wonderful after-hour events with friends in the DC night life, after concerts in the park at places like Carter Barron (Rock Creek Park) and Fort Dupont, after holding great leadership positions in my field, I decided to go back to Cincinnati in 2005 risking my status, salary, and lifestyle (much to the chagrin of many of my D.C. friends on the east coast... and now I truly understand their hesitation and concern).

Chapter 13:

A Strange Homecoming

*"The Lord God hath given me the tongue of the learned, that I should know how to speak a word in season to him that is weary; he wakeneth morning by morning, he wakeneth mine ear to hear as the learned. The Lord God hath opened mine ear, and I was not rebellious, neither turned away back. I gave my back to the smiters, and my cheeks to them that plucked off the hair: I hid not my face from shame and spitting. For the Lord God will help me; therefore, shall I not be confounded; therefore, have I set my face like a flint, and I know that I shall not be ashamed." – **Isaiah 50: 4-7**

My Aunt Chick was living alone, getting older, and needing more direct care. So, I started circulating my resume for jobs back in Cincinnati, knowing I would probably have to take a pay-cut or take a position of a lower level than my current Director position. I was willing to sacrifice that for being back with Aunt Chick and my family in Ohio. Besides, Julia was only four, and I wanted her to get to know some of her cousins and other family members. After four months of a heated search for jobs in Cincinnati, Ohio, the children's hospital relocated me (and my daughter) back home. It was a very precious time that we spent with family, but challenging for me in the professional arena there. It appears that as I have aged, I now sound exactly like my sister Cecilia. I was hired as an Education & Development Specialist position (I did have to take a dip in title and salary), and was assigned to teach the bi-weekly New Hire Orientation (to new hires, and audience of 100-120 persons) as well as teach other professional development subjects to the current staff of the hospital. When I began delivering training at Cultural Diversity was a hot topic, and I had to teach about 3 4-hour courses on this subject there weekly. One day after I first started, I was about to begin a session of Cultural Diversity & Inclusion class there, and a nurse from the audience shouted at me "you must be Cecilia's sister!" I was stunned, as I had never met this woman before in my life. Ceal's daughter has sickle cell, and Brittany has been a patient for many years, sometimes for very difficult situations with her illness. So, apparently Ceal's voice was a familiar one for this nurse who worked the sickle cell unit there. But the fact that she called me out like so, really told me I definitely have the same deep, gruffy voice that my sister Cecilia has, which for me is also often mistaken for a man's voice via telephone.

It's ironic that Cultural Diversity was one of the subjects that I taught *(again, God puts us where we need to be)*, because it is a subject that I have been challenged with personally (with my own heritage and appearance). I would start some courses and say, "Look at me – I am the case for diversity!" Here in Cincinnati, I wanted to push more D&I (Diversity & Inclusion) in my training like I did at Providence Hospital in DC, because I have seen how educating and training staff on this subject helps them work together smoothly and has so many other great outcomes. In the workplace, when employees have a greater understanding of their co-workers who are "different" than them, there is less fear, less intimidation, and less hesitancy to work together, whatever the task at hand. This not only works on the job, but it also works in real life. I've seen it repeatedly through teaching languages (English and Spanish), and definitely through teaching about safety practices. Through more communication and understanding of language, culture, history, and human nature, we all can be more productive when we encounter one another if all these "differences" are leveled, explained, understood, and respected.

I had the honor of leading a team of Human Resources (HR) and Training professionals to re-design the hospital's 8-hour Cultural Diversity Orientation program, converting it into a 30-minute web-based training program. Dr. Ian Barrett (HR Assistant Vice President at the time) tapped me (who was working in the Training Department) to guide the team through the re-design process. The team included other training professionals like Richard Gardner (Instructional Designer), Sonya Wallace (Diversity Trainer), and Steven

Baines (Diversity Trainers), and after a house-wide survey and four months of data analysis and web-based instructional design work, the team created the new learning module for orientation that was more accurate, more engaging, took less time (key to hospital staff), and was online. Ironically, at this time, I was also assigned to teach a LOT of Conflict Resolution classes across the hospital. I definitely had my training work cut out for me, but it was all very gratifying knowing that I was up to the challenge to design and deliver it all effectively for so many people.

This team also re-designed the annual mandatory Cultural Diversity classes for the current staff of the hospital from 8 hours to 4 hours in the classroom, so they still had to attend in-person training on this subject, which brought about the opportunity for hospital staff to discuss some real D&I issues face-to-face. Steven, Sonya, and I covered all of the delivery of the Diversity Training, and it was an interesting endeavor every time I (we) taught a class at the hospital – SO many interesting stories of both love *and* hate (really misunderstandings) for those who were/are different than themselves. We would show the video of Miss Jane Elliott's "Blue-Eyed, Brown-Eyed Experiment", and would facilitate the interesting and unique dialogue that would come from each group. And being a green-eyed Black woman, I not only got lots of questions about *my* eye color and its origin, but we had lots of interesting dialogue about how physical appearances in humans can be deceptive and hindering until you get to know that person (some have preconceptions/assumptions before they get to know me – I learned to NOT do that to others). I even taught my daughter some of these lessons of D&I, repeatedly showing her the cute HBO video "Happy to Be Nappy", which she still recalls to this day as a nice memory (and she's 20 years old now). I felt very blessed that God should place me in this role in my life at this time. This training team did a great thing for the hospital and their staff: we helped the employees understand the importance of working together more harmoniously (and that could only be by making efforts to get to know one another despite personal differences), and taught the employees how to greet and care for all individuals and families visiting the hospital per their unique, diverse needs demonstrating their cultural competency.

I continued teaching and facilitating the Cultural Diversity & Inclusion training at this hospital, leading a lot of interesting conversations between all races about the importance of respecting those who are different than we are. After speaking with class participants that are from Kentucky and Indiana particularly, I have learned that many families in this region of the U.S. (and all over the country really) struggle with racial issues *generationally.* And as much as I tried to deliver the message of Cultural Diversity, Equity, & Inclusion (CDE&I), there is still someone out there teaching about hate to counter my effort. Sometimes it felt exhausting to teach about CDE&I in Cincinnati (especially when I was experiencing racial hatred directly in my beloved hometown myself, personally and professionally). It left me torn between my own sanity and health, and trying to fight this battle against those who I know systematically have more power than me. No matter how I tried to level the playing field among all these micro-aggressions against me as an intelligent Black female (and as a single mother), there was just too much stacked against me. It was a battle I would never win, and in this, ironically, I knew just how my father felt about the "pressures" of living and trying to thrive in Cincinnati, Ohio. I was teaching about positive things that we all should do to respect our neighbors more, but I could not see it happening to me and to my people in real life out in my community.

It would sadden me to coincidentally run into some of my neighborhood buddies with whom I grew up in Evanston who were, now instead, on the street corner asking me for money. Although I knew many from St. Mark who have prospered there in Cincinnati, this hurt me to know that just as many did not and were struggling to live now. I did not want to turn out the same way, so I wanted to retreat from Cincinnati... again. Additionally, as much as we, the final parishioners of St. Mark tried to avoid it, we were all heart-broken when the Archdiocese of Cincinnati closed St. Mark and forced parishioners to attend the "Church of the Resurrection" in Bond Hill merging three other Cincinnati parishes that had also closed (St. Andrew's on Reading Road, St. Agnes, and St. Francis De Salles on Madison Road). I felt like the needs of the Black community were not being heard in Cincinnati; as hard as I trained on "bridging the gap" it was all so discouraging. One good thing that came out of my re-connection with St. Mark is that I served as a member of the Board of Directors for Alliance Academy of Cincinnati (formerly St. Mark Catholic Elementary School, now a charter school owned by National Heritage Academies). A Xavier University Professor Emeritus named Dr. Timothy Kloppenborg with whom I taught Project Management at Children's Hospital nominated my name to Mrs. Kathleen Gallon (Board President at the time in 2005). This was very rewarding to know that I was giving back to St. Mark by serving to improve and maintain it.

At the same time, my namesake's situation was getting more challenging as she insisted on living on her own in her apartment on Montgomery Road right across from St. Mark Catholic Church. My sisters Karen, Cecilia, and I shared checking in on her daily to make sure she did not have soured food in her refrigerator, taking out her trash regularly, bringing her what she needed, tidying up her sur-roundings, and checking with her neighbors on her well-being. She still became the victim of a "bad landlord" who let her building get run down and avoided paying utilities in a timely fashion. Some days the heat would go out in winter, and she would be there with a space heater (which scared us to no end). Or other times in the summer, she would not turn on the air conditioner my brother Carl would put in her window each season, but instead we would find her inside listening to Reverend Al Sharpton on the radio while having a single fan blowing hot air on her instead (both of which she found comforting). Being a child of the Depression, she knew how to live on less than the basics of life, and we could not understand why she did not want to take on these "modern comforts of life" that we were offering her. She never wanted anything "extra". Her building had to be condemned for the landlord's lack of attention, and all residents were asked to leave by a certain date. We arranged for Aunt Chick to be put in a nursing facility in Avondale (where Mom's friend Miss Mamie Beal, who lived on Dauner in Evanston, also resided and I visited her regularly with my daughter Julia). Aunt Chick, never wanting to leave her nest of over 50 years, did not like it and was in a lot of arthritic pain when she arrived. She died four days later, and may her soul rest in peace. Although it was heart-breaking to see our family matriarch go, I was glad to have spent her last six years on the planet in her presence with my daughter.

I learned many lessons from my enigmatic homecoming return to Cincinnati, Ohio, and one main lesson was that I learned more about me and how I feel about myself. I learned to enjoy and cherish faith, family, and life, and let no one steal your joy whomever they may be. I know that regardless of my rocky past, I must continue to lead and share these lessons, and be a wise guide to those after me to help them avoid the pitfalls of life (as many have done for me). I must continue to "bridge the gap" and bring people together, as I am known to do, especially diverse groups of people to facilitate collaboration and good dialogue among God's people instead of so much conflict. If I can bring people of different languages together, and help them communicate, I feel like I have stepped up my game in my mission! Learning and speaking a foreign language has allowed me to meet people from all over the world, and has made me realize that much responsibility comes with this platform and with my dialogue. Yes, it has empowered me to speak in two tongues, but *what* I say and how I use my language capability is very important. I must always use my platform to display positivity, unity of humanity (regardless of our backgrounds), and love. I forever plan to be the change that I would like to see, because I know that starts with me.

(Listen to the song "Be the Change We Want to See" by Jarrod Lawson.)

Another lesson that I learned from all this is to appreciate one another more, especially those who are different than me. Per Benjamin Franklin, "Nothing is certain but death and taxes." Others say that "the three certainties of life are birth, death, and change". They're all constant over which we all have no control; they continually occur and are cyclical. We too have to realize that life is cyclical, and that it is indeed precious… every day of it. And each day God gives us a chance to better ourselves, our communities, our country, and our planet. Each person should have the opportunity to live his/her best life, as we care for each other. Yes, we are our brother's keeper! We should find ways (everyday) to help others, those who are not living their best life. We should not sit comfortably "when we get ours", and do nothing while our neighbor blocks away go to sleep hungry in a cold home worrying about what tomorrow might bring. We surely need better coordination on this across our country, but if everyone took up a "cause" out there (and we have many in our country, hunger is a big one) and were committed to helping *anyone* who is in need, we would have fewer social issues across our country. Many of the current issues are really unnecessary for such a bountiful country. I pledge to use my God-given talents to do nothing but uplift humanity and help my fellow man or woman whenever I am able. This, I have discovered, is part of my mission too. Those "angels" on your path are great to have, but God sometimes places those "strangers" before us as opportunities to show His love through our actions and how we might treat one another (hopefully we'll use those opportunities positively). When we, adversely, show hate toward one another, it has disastrous effects on our lives, our communities, on our country, and on our planet. Brothers and sisters: **LOVE is the way!**

> *"Beloved, if God so loved us, we ought also to love one another. No man hath seen God at any time. If we love one another, God dwelleth in us, and His love is perfected in us."* – *I John 4:11-13*

Chapter 14:
Coming Full Circle

A fter my Aunt Naomi (Chick's) death, I felt depleted from so many unnecessary personal and professional racially-driven challenges at work and home, and felt like my mission of caring for my namesake had ended. So, seven years after my return home to Cincinnati, I sold my beautiful home, took another leap of faith, and my daughter and I returned to the DC area for the possibility of a bit more professional growth, opportunity, and multiculturalism. Before I left, Kathleen Gallon and the Board of Directors of Alliance Academy of Cincinnati awarded me with an Appreciation for Distinguished Service Award for working with the board to improve the school academics, staff, and physical grounds. The honor to work with them was all mine really.

I was eager to return to the DC area, and so were many of my Delta sorors and friends. And once again, I would be near my sister Angela and cousin Theodora "Teddy" Calloway (on the Robinson side of my family). I did not move back into the District of Columbia, because DC's real estate pricing had skyrocketed and gentrification was/is occurring at a rapid pace there. So, I paced myself in my transition back to the east coast by moving into a city just over the DC line in Prince George's County, MD. Here I have been able to connect with many of my CSU college buddies, and I currently am part of the DC CSU Alumni Chapter, actively recruiting and raising funds for scholarships for current CSU students.

When I first returned to the "DMV" area, again it was teaching English and Spanish that helped me pay my rent until I got hired by a prestigious inner-city university in DC as a Health & Safety Training Specialist, ironically, designing and delivering mandatory OSHA (Occupational Safety & Health Administration) and EPA (Environmental Protection Agency) safety training to the operational staff of the university in both English and Spanish (they had a substantial number of Latino employees doing grounds work, electrical work, carpentry, Housekeeping, etc. managing the university operations. I went on to take on another leadership position in training at a large health insurance company, supervising Trainers across the US. It was another great opportunity to share my knowledge, skills, and experiences with those new to training and instructional design, but it also presented the opportunity to be a leader in decision-making and being a role model to diverse groups of people on how to "get along". Again, in whatever position or title I have held or any others that I will ever hold, I am now sure that God places me *exactly* where I need to be. I now trust that whole-heartedly. At this point I began to join my brother Fran's weekly Bible studies, and that gave me the opportunity for even more personal introspection into God's Word and His purpose for me.

But look at me now, searching through the past for lost memories, for closure, and for treasures that would allow me to better know and love my father the way a daughter should. Searching for clues on how he lived, to understand him better and the "pressures" he experienced, and what got him to the point of making the final "dark" decision that he made that greatly affected me and my siblings - the reasons why. "How could you let this happen, Daddy... why? Did something happen to you as *you* grew up in your large family that made you feel that you had to do this? Did all nine of us drive you to the point of wanting to take your own life? Why did you decide to leave Mom alone like that when you *both* brought all of us into this world? And why did you do that *when* you did it in 1966?" I probably will only find just that: clues... and never the real answers. But it's something that I had to do to try to fill in some of the gaps of my mind where he was not. "What really happened to him? Did he caress my hair like Mom did when I was little? Did he love me like all my other siblings or did he get to nine (looking at me) and question himself and not want any more children?" These are all typical questions of someone surviving suicide, and trying to imagine what was going through that suicide victim's mind at the time of their death... especially if it occurred as a young person.

I never got a chance to dialogue with my father like my siblings did. I heard some about this from Mom (having experienced more of her in my life than him). Ever since arriving in Cincinnati (and definitely beforehand) there was a longing that I had like never before to come back home to Cincinnati to "find" him and my memories of him. And so, for these reasons, the "strange homecoming to Cincinnati" was worth it. I lost the memories of him and Mom at such an early age (painful to this day), that it's hard to remember the finer things about either of them. So, for this I live vicariously through my siblings and the other members of my family. I really wrote a lot of this to satisfy my desire to fill that gap of the memories of them both.

Many of my friends (and my sister Angela especially) said I was crazy to leave Washington, D.C. after 20 years and return home to conservative, prejudiced Cincinnati. "They've rioted there over race for years, and it's clear that it's still a major issue for the city. I think you're regressing" my sister Angela told me. Well, she was probably right, but I had to try it for several reasons: I had to come back to help my namesake "Aunt Chick" go into her last days; I'm SO grateful that I did that to share her last five years on the planet with her. I also had to come back to my siblings and their kids so that my daughter could grow up and experience all the fun with all her cousins like I did growing up. But I really was drawn to go back to search my roots and try to bring some closure to what happened to father's life, and I knew that I could only find some of those answers in Cincinnati, Ohio where it all happened. I was not able to do so after the death of my mom, focusing on college and after moving to DC *(one of the best decisions I've made in my life)*, but I always had that "hole in my heart" to learn more about Cincinnati and my family's (my parents') history there.

Now after having returned to Cincinnati and left again, I understand the "madness" that Daddy must have experienced here. It must have been really hard to have been "Black Like Me" *(as Mickey Guyton sings in her song of the same name)* back in the 1960s especially, as I was experiencing the same thing he did after the turn of the 21st century. Depriving a person of their basic human rights and privileges really can drive a person crazy. I learned that all over again in Cincinnati when I returned, and I'm not even a Black *man (I know it is worse for the Black man)*. To not be respected for your skills, talents, and abilities, I'm sure, contributed to his insanity and eventual diagnosis of schizophrenia. Sometimes I, myself, have felt insane with the way I was treated when I returned home, particularly in the working world (in comparison to how I've been revered and respected professionally in the Washington, D.C. area). Some whites (in Cincinnati and in other cities back in the 60s and to this day) believe that Blacks cannot possibly be intelligent enough to lead and/or be in charge of *anything*. They should not be allowed to think on their own; someone must think for them. This has given me a feeling of disempowerment and lacking control over my life (hard after being what I felt was in full control of my life in another setting).

Similar to my father, I have felt that my world was spinning out of control while living in Cincinnati, and that I could do nothing about it. Again, those micro-aggressions set in, and there were so many unseen forces against me that I could not battle. There were so many unwritten rules and procedures that we must follow in order to be "in good" in the eyes of our white counterparts. The things that we must accept (that we really don't want to or don't believe in) in order to be able to hold down a good job and tolerate the intolerable in corporate America. Often times you don't know that you've even done anything wrong until it's too late. But when you try to take initiative or to lead, that's when you find out that "you've overstepped your bounds" (something I was told before by a supervisor). I've been told a lot of times (especially by Aunt Chick and other family members that have never left Cincinnati): "You just can't do that in Cincinnati." "No one wants to hear your opinion. It won't matter anyway."

I imagine how it probably was equally hard for Daddy dealing with the Cincinnati culture and the racially tense culture of the entire country during the 60s. It must have been hard for him to have been bi-racial in appearance, leaving him to "pass" as being white enough, but other times not being black enough to those in his own community. Never white enough and never black enough (the same thing I grew up experiencing, but probably not nearly as bad as he had it). I often felt the same, torn between races because of my appearance and constantly walking the "color line." I've been told by many "that they (whites) accept you more, Naomi, because you look like them." But those blacks who tell me that don't know that I (and my dad did also) receive all of the same prejudices that any other black would receive and sometimes more (because of how we looked). My daughter even told me that her classmates asked about me: "Is your Mom white?" And she would have to explain that I'm Black, but just look different. My daughter told me that she felt like she was treated "better" because her Mom looked white. I didn't know how to receive that but to tell her that "This is America, babe."

Similar to my father (and mother), my appearance stands out among blacks, and I'm definitely not white. But in Cincinnati, I would often get the "Who the Hell does she think she is?" look from whites AND from some blacks! And I'm sure my father got the same thing when he exuded even a *bit* of confidence in whatever he did. But often in the past, it was actually many fair-skinned and bi-racial blacks that helped ALL blacks enjoy the privileges that they have today (along with the suffering of all the other blacks). History in America indicates that groups like Jack and Jill, and black fraternities and sororities started as social groups with members that had fair-skin or those who could pass the "paper bag" test (being lighter than a brown paper bag). If you read the book "Our Kind of People" by Lawrence Otis Graham, historically, some of the political maneuvers and social actions of many of these minority social groups were more accepted by whites then. They actually helped break down barriers for *everyone* in the Black community, and they began to be accepted where

Blacks had not been allowed before (some only because they "passed" like my father. Those individuals were actually ground-breaking for their time.

When I think back on the Blacks in Evanston, many of them were also ground-breaking, and they really ALL are the "Kids of King", in how they persevered and navigated through so much social turmoil that exists then and still persists to this day. But on the other hand, we were also so influenced by Evanston, our local community, and the musical sounds we listened to (from King Records and beyond). As we grew up in "that bubble" among all the turmoil of the times, the tunes often helped us navigate the struggle. There are SO many memories that get sparked from those tunes. Cincinnati, Evanston, the sounds of King Records, the many artists there, many (like my father) who came from the local community are still a treasure to the city.

Some things in Cincinnati really have changed since I've lived there in the 60s, 70s, and 80s. At one point, no one like me was allowed to move into North College Hill... *at all*. But I lived there with my daughter in a beautiful home. I try to remain optimistic about what more could change for the positive there. However, some racial things haven't changed in Cincinnati (like many major cities and their black communities). In the city where I currently live in MD, they actually changed the name of the local park, because at one time that person set an ordinance that "the park was to be used by its white residents only."

Much is changing in America, but some things seem like they never will. Racial injustice and inequality are flaws that will continue to hold our country back from being the great country that it can be. Many things in Cincinnati have changed since I was a little girl growing up there, but Cincinnati's love of good food and good down-home music has never changed; I don't think it ever will. Technology, fast-paced living, a growing citizenship and growing commuter population, and increased business demands have kept Cincinnati's name on the map of major cities in the Midwest, and it is still a wonderful place to visit.

And my relocation back to Cincinnati was actually good for me and my personal search to find out more about Naomi. And yes, it also allowed me to do a lot of research (specifically in the Cincinnati library) about my family history and about King Records. Ever since I've returned to DC, I have continued researching my family's history and asking my family, friends, neighbors, and any fellow-Cincinnatian I could talk to and ask questions like **"What was the culture of our local community in Evanston like as we grew up on Grantwood Avenue in the mid-sixties and seventies? How did the ever-conservative Cincinnati culture influence me personally and/or professionally in my life? How have some of the tragedies that my family has experienced affected my life/our lives?"** These are just some of the questions I've been asking for a long time, but the recent Insurrection at the nation's Capital Building in January 2021, and all of our recent social unrest (Black Lives Matter protests from George Floyd's death) have prompted me to write this book, and has provided me with some introspection regarding my role in this issue that will obviously outlive me. These are just some of the questions that I had hoped to answer in this exposé of my family, my life, and more specifically about my mother and father, particularly my father, since I did not get a chance to know either of them very well. I felt like I was missing some important information about my life that most people are also naturally curious about: where they came from and how much of those roots are in them. I wanted/want to know more in this regard. This journey through my past has quenched some of that thirst for knowing more about my family's past, but I'm always curious to know more. However, this walk through, this analysis of my past has indeed brought me some closure and healing in many ways, the healing and closure that I (and probably my entire family and many other families) have needed for many years after their loss.

Sadly, one thing I cannot change, is the racial division and mental illness (sometimes one leading to the other) that still occurs too frequently and often unnecessarily across our great country. We only need to love and respect one another more to get to this seemingly utopian place for our country, but I believe that it is possible – but God must be in the picture... include Him always! Our people, our communities, and our country lose out when we don't focus on God's intent for us to *love one another*. I love Cincinnati and I hate what we went through growing up there, but these facts of life (suicide, loss, mental illness, racial injustice) are everywhere. But I know in my heart that fewer losses would occur among us if in society we love and care for each other more. My siblings and I always received a lot of love there in spite of these challenges we faced. We grew up in our "bubble of protection" within the village of Evanston and our St. Mark community while there was truly a lot of crazy things happening all around us in Cincinnati and out in the big world back in the 60s and 70s, more than we ever realized.

However, many things in Cincinnati have not changed at all that keep it perceived as behind the times... many things have stayed exactly the same. There are a host of jokes out there about how behind the city is in comparison to other major U.S. cities. Tom Sawyer is quoted as saying, "If the world ends, I want to be in Cincinnati, because it'll happen to them seven years later!" Everyone says Cincinnati is late to come of age with what is happening in the rest of the country, which is why so many of my friends and family questioned my desire to return back home to Cincinnati. Some say it can be stuck in its unique conservative heritage, lifestyle, and way of thinking. But it also is a very beautiful, family-oriented river city with its own old-fashioned local charm. It is truly middle America; it's apple pie. That's what draws me back there and keeps me returning, not to mention the vast majority of my family is there. But now, I truly understand a whole lot more about the city of Cincinnati and the interesting events that have formed its story-filled history. It is indeed a beautiful landscape, whether you're looking at it from Eden Park, from Bellevue Park, from

Fort Washington, or the amazing "skyline" vista you see driving on I-75 North through the hillsides of northern Kentucky approaching Cincinnati... truly a "Queen City". Many during the 1940's said that the view of the Ohio river from Cincinnati's Eden Park looked like living in Germany, looking "Over-the-Rhine" River (where the famous title "Over-the-Rhine" came from for the community in downtown Cincinnati). But, like many cities in America, this city (and many cities nationwide) needs to take a closer look at equities for all people and work toward "bridging the gap" more.

I am still hopeful and inspired, and willing to do my part in trying to make all our communities stronger, more productive, and more loving. All this has been enlightening, and I am indeed at a point of greater understanding that have discovered my mission in life: to bring persons of all backgrounds together and teach them how to work well together to do whatever they need to do to make this planet a better place. I will surely continue to design, develop, and deliver skill-based training, but also teach *more* of the "soft skills" like basic communication skills, some cultural diversity, lots more conflict resolution, heck even some faith and LOVE training!

I'm glad I decided to have my life extend beyond Ohio (and beyond America). Some parts of my history in Ohio hurt to think about, but I should not forget it because it makes me who I am today. And the painful points in my life have actually awakened my faith in God. Some things about my upbringing will never leave my heart and mind (the good and the bad – I must accept both). My treasured history goes with me, and I have learned to cherish all aspects of this "wonderful life" and all that has come with it (even the painful stuff). My roots and my family's roots and history are there forever, and ironically, I'll never stop returning to that because I know that it also encompasses so much love received from my "village" there. I will definitely always come back to Cincinnati for those cheese coneys! *(note: a "cheese coney" is a hot dog with mustard, chili, and cheese that is traditional to Cincinnati cuisine – delicious!)*

> *"The righteous cry, and the Lord heareth, and delivereth them out of all of their troubles. The lord is nigh unto them that are of a broken heart; and saveth such as be of a contrite spirit. Many are the afflictions of the righteous; but the Lord delivereth him out of them all." –* ***Psalms 34: 17-19***

Chapter 15 :

Epilogue –
From a Mess to a Mission

I am a living testimony of God's love through others. So many "angels" have crossed my path making it smoother along my way in life (my siblings at the forefront of this group). So many "miracles" have occurred to hold me over to my present state in life that I must testify that God has worked through many wonderful people to make Naomi who she is today. I acknowledged this in my teens, and ever since have been grateful for those who have helped me in life, especially when I most needed it. And I plan to provide the same level of assistance to others who cross my path in need, especially young women of color like I was when I experienced so many of life's challenges. People are still shocked and amazed when I tell them that I lost both of my parents by 16 years old, and some don't know how to react to me or what I've just told them. Sometimes there is that awkward silence, or I get a double-take from them. Some are empathetic and understanding, expressing their pride in how far I've come managing all the loss in my history and all the emotions that come from it (they still do, to this day). For me it only takes a photo, a memorable song, or an old memento from one of my parents that can trigger a rainstorm of tears about their short lives. But I still have so much pride for my parents and the family heritage and faith they have raised in us, and this makes me focus on our good memories. My siblings and I are all very blessed and accomplished now, and we try to share that "joie de vie" and our strong faith with others, since we definitely have experience in life's struggles. We are ever committed to one another, faithful in our support of each other, and always gotta call each other "just to check in"… a blessing that many don't have and I never take for granted.

But life has truly been difficult for me, especially as a young teenager… "it ain't been no crystal stair" as Langston Hughes stated. So, I end this book with a message of faith and testimony during this (what appears to be subsiding) pandemic season. Look at God; He can get us through anything! During this time of pandemic and social unrest in this country this message of **love, perseverance, and faith** is much needed at this time in the world. Now, of all times in my life, I know and realize that there is a lesson from God at the end of everything I (we) do, which is why this chapter summary is duly titled. I personally went from being in a very messy situation (two of them if you consider the death of each parent at a young age), but God turned that into a Mission for me. Daily as I do my morning meditations and prayer, I wait for God to speak to me to show me guidance through my continually challenging life, and He has always done so, and always helped me to land softly throughout my life, whatever I am experiencing. I am truly blessed for all of the "angels" (Mom and Daddy especially) that have lighted my path, held me, comforted me, and protected me throughout my tragic and difficult young life. I'm sure that these same "angels" are still always present with me and with my daughter Julia, protecting us from all of the evil, hate, and treachery that will forever be present in our world (and which we see so clearly present day even). Angels hold a great theme for me in my life. They have helped sustain me and make me what I am today. So, I say, in conclusion, **thank you God** for having all of these angels come my way, and for all those You have yet to send. They are the reason why I am still here… in whatever city/location I'll be regardless of my situation in life. And please help me to be an angel for others (Your working hands here on earth) to assist others who might be going through similar circumstances.

Everyone always says **"God will not put more on you than you can handle."** Well, he must think I'm pretty strong, because I've had some very trying times in my life, particularly in my teen years dealing with so much loss. My testimony and the source of my strength to get through every life challenge is to **keep close to the Father (God), the Son (Jesus), and allowing the Holy Spirit and his Holy Word to guide you in your life**. This is what me and my siblings have done over the years to persevere, survive, and succeed in life, and many look up to us as a group for our strong faith, unity, and family-oriented values (true to our Midwest roots).

As I conclude, I share with you some quotes that have been particularly inspirational, are memorable, helpful, and those that I have used often as affirmations to get me through some really tough times throughout my life. Sometimes, I occasionally like to just crack open the Bible at any point and see what message God has for me in that instance... often times the message I read is on point for what I needed at the time. I want to testify to everyone that through faith in God, *all* things are possible even when I couldn't see it in the moment, and I have learned from experience to keep the faith; God will always deliver on your prayers and on His promises.

After surviving my father's suicide, after the experience of being an orphan at 16, after losing my mother and both of my grandmothers within 18 months I was lost, con-fused, hurting badly, and full of gloom about my future in the world (like my father). But praise God, through the love of my dear siblings, many mentors, neighbors in my Evanston community, and from my school and church, I found the support I needed. I was never really alone in the world as I felt then; God has been parenting me all along through others. God worked through all these people (this "village") to help me survive my painful circumstances. And although I still feel the pain of all this today, I now know how to handle and vent it properly so that it does not overcome me like it did when I was young. Yes, I have experienced much loss, but I feel triumphant along with my siblings and confident in how the Lord has and currently holds us in His mighty and capable hands. Stating that "God truly pulled me through a rough patch in life" is truly an understatement.

My brother Fran recently sent an affirmation of the Word on **10/12/2020** (which he does on our family and Bible study group chat), and it stated: *"When life surprises us, whether that surprise is about the birth of a child, an unforeseen health problem, an accident, a raving success, or what appears to be an untimely death, none of it takes God by surprise. When life shocks us, we can **lay back in God's arms** and trust that He has a plan for us. God's ultrasound pieces through the gloom of sin and sees a bright future for each of us, if only we believe." So,* I had to learn to "lay back in God's arms" and trust in Him in all things and lean on His Holy Word.

I have always prayed intently with my family members; we do so shamelessly. But since I joined my brother Fran's weekly Bible study in 2019 in fellowship with some other Christian friends of the family, it has been guiding, consoling, and comforting to my soul. It has kept me at peace, and maintained my spirits during this recent global pandemic. Fran has kept us all in continual prayer and close to the Word of God, and it has been invaluable for me and many others. I encourage anyone reading this now to join a Bible study and/or prayer group also to keep you close to the Word of God. The crazier this world has gotten since I have joined, the more I am glad that I made that choice to join others in fellowship and prayer regularly. We also stay in a constant state of gratitude while we read the Word, finding encouragement every time we read and review together. We pray for ourselves and for others, and we learn about how to govern ourselves in a positive Christian way during our daily routines to be a good example to others. The weekly Bible study has been continually leading me, especially as I conclude this book. Our country is experiencing a host of issues, among them, a global pandemic and great social, political, and racial unrest. We *all* need more of the Word of God in our lives to guide us in all that we do to maintain our moral compass. So, grab a Bible, follow along, get to reading (in fellowship with others), and you, too, will receive the peace, faith, and strength that will get you through life's difficulties as well!

To get you started, I share with you here some of my favorite biblical quotations for inspiration – those that I use continually to get me through any challenging time. Stay blessed:

> **Psalm 23 –** This quote hangs in my house and is a regular go-to biblical quote for strength – *"The Lord is my Shephard; I shall not want..."*

> **Matthew 11:28-30 –** *"Come unto Me, all ye that labor and are heavy laden, and I will give you rest. Take my Yoke upon you, and <u>learn</u> of me; for I am meek and lowly in heart; and ye shall find rest unto*

your souls. For my Yoke is easy, and my burden is light."

Psalm 91:1-11 – *"He that dwelleth in the secret place of the most-High shall abide under the shadow of the Almighty. I will say of the Lord, He is my refuge and my fortress: my God in Him I will trust. Surely, He shall deliver thee from the snare of the fowler, and from the pestilence. He shall cover thee with his feathers, and under his wings shalt though trust: His truth shall be thy shield and buckler. Though shalt not be afraid for the terror by night; nor for the arrow that flieth by day. Nor the pestilence that walketh in darkness; nor for the destruction that wasteth at noonday. A thousand shall fall by thy side, and ten thousand at thy right hand; but it shall not come nigh thee. Only with thine eyes shalt though behold and seethe reward of the wicked. Because thou hast made the Lord, which is my refuge, even the most-High, thy habitation. There shall no evil befall thee, neither shall any plague come nigh thy dwelling. For He shall give his angels charge over thee, to keep thee in all thy ways."*

Ruth 4:14 – *"Then the women said to Naomi, 'Blessed be the Lord, who has not left you this day without a close relative (NIV says guardian–redeemer), and may his name be famous in Israel."*

(Naomi clung to Ruth and Boaz, persevered, and in the end prospered.)

Proverbs 22:6 – *"Train up a child in the way he should go: and when he is old, he will not depart from it."*

Trusting in God that my needs are always met: Philippians 4:12-14 – *(this came up during mass on 10/11/20 at St. Augustine Catholic Church in DC)* A Letter of St. Paul to the Philippians: *"Brothers and sisters, **I know** how to live in humble circumstances; I know also how to live with abundance. In every circumstance and in all things, I have learned the secret of being well-fed and of going hungry, of living in abundance and of being in need. I can do all things in Him who strengthens me. Still, it was kind of you of you to share in my distress. My God will fully supply whatever you need, in accord with His glorious riches in Christ Jesus. To our God and Father, glory forever and ever. Amen."*

I Corinthians 10:31 – *"Whether therefore you eat, or drink, or whatsoever ye do, do all to the Glory of God."*

Psalm 100 – *"Make a joyful noise unto the Lord, all ye lands. Serve the Lord with gladness: come before His presence with singing. Know that the Lord He is God: It is he that hath made us, and not we ourselves; we are His people, and the sheep of* *his pasture. Enter into His gates with thanksgiving, and into his courts with praise: be thankful unto Him, and bless His name. For the Lord is good; his mercy is everlasting; and his truths endureth to all generations."*

Besides all the support I received in my teen years from my church members of St. Mark, friends at Ursuline Academy of Cincinnati (my high school**), I want to specifically thank my late brother Robert Kinney, Jr. – "Bobby"** first for bringing me close to the Word particularly in my teen years which helped me maneuver so much grief then. So many others have supported me in my growth in faith in my life (if I was open to receiving it), and showed me how to cling to my faith and to trust God in every valley. I would not be where I am now having such a fulfilling life without this support of faith throughout my life. **Secondly, I thank my brother, Rev. Francis Wayne Kinney**, (here later in life) who continually helps me keep perspective on the importance of God's Word in my life. He has taught me that, regarding the Word of God, you must do three key things:

- **Know** the Word (study/learn it)

- **Believe** in the Word (even for those things not seen, maintain trust in God/His Word)

- **Act** on the Word! (you must share it with others and spread the Good News!)

Both of these honorable men have often served as my father growing up without one. But now that I look back,

I believe that God was still "parenting me" all the while... but through them and all my siblings! We are God's hands! One thing I have learned is that through God all things are possible, and when in the valley He will work you back to the mountain-top, but you must **maintain your faith, be grateful to God and trust in the power of His Holy Trinity and His Word.** I always try to show this life's lesson to my daughter Julia day to day.

I plan to continue to use my platform of being an Instructor/ Trainer/Mentor/Speaker/Writer for over thirty years to share the Word of God (and somehow the opportunity always presents itself - blessings!). I will continue to be a comfort to those "strangers" who cross my path, because God has comforted me so over time (often through others). Now my "mission" is to continually be "His vessel" and "His hands" to work through me to help others who were in similar circumstances as me or who just need my help (particularly young women of color who don't always get the opportunities they deserve).

Luke 10:25-37 is *the story of the Good Samaritan* helping the man overcome by robbers when traveling from Jerusalem to Jericho. A priest passed the beat-up man, then a Levite passed him by too, but it was the (lowly, looked down upon) Samaritan who took the time to help the man – he stopped, tended to his wounds, helped him get off the road, AND paid out of his pocket at the inn for the guy to have a place to stay overnight to heal. How many of us look for that person along the side of the road?

Mother Theresa stated that "in the face of the poor and helpless is Jesus".... Look closer at those in need; it could be your call from God to help! We all can reach out and help others with the gifts God has given us. This is my life's mission: to share my knowledge, my skills, and <u>definitely my faith</u> with others.

Fran also sent another affirmation of the Word on **10/28/2020** that stated: *"Maybe you heard the Christian cliché 'God can turn your mess into a message'. It may sound cheesy, but it's true! The Lord uses our pain, our stories, our history to help others along the way. We are comforted so we can give comfort. Suffering can enrich us with wisdom and compassion so that we can help others. How have you seen that in your life?"*

(And then he referenced in a text) **II Corinthians: 2-4 which states –** *"May God our Father and the Lord Jesus Christ give you grace and peace. All praise to God the Father of our Lord Jesus Christ. God is our merciful Father and the source of all comfort. He comforts us in all our troubles so that we can comfort others. When they are troubled, we will be able to give them the same comfort God has given us. For the more we suffer for Christ, the more God will shower us with His comfort through Christ. Even when we are weighed down with troubles, it is for your comfort and salvation!".*

My life was a mess indeed, and I *still* hurt over the fact that I lost my parents so very young and had to navigate my own life at such a young age. **I *used to* ask "Why ME?"**

But now I know why: "Why NOT you, Naomi? He is calling you toward your (His) mission. Answer!" It is truly God's will, and I have learned to accept it and follow it as my purpose in my life... what He would have me do. The answer is also because God knew (but I surely didn't know then) that I would eventually become strong enough to handle the load and, in turn, I would lead others (His children of God) by example. But staying close to the Word and leaning on my faith my whole life has now brought me great peace in life and I now clearly hear the message! **My life now has true purpose, meaning, and a mission. I now ask myself "In spite of life's challenges, how can I be that example of perseverance, empowerment, and fortitude to others, especially those with minimal resources? How can I be the vessel through which Your Word, O Lord, and wisdom are conveyed which always ends in goodness and blessings abound?" The answer is to share the examples of where I have been blessed, and to show that hard times in life will come (sometimes soon in life), but they are indeed surmountable. And my faith and my family have definitely been there to help carry me through.** I could go on and on about how God has been my Refuge, my Rock, my Messenger, and my Comfort in good and bad times in my life. I think the "Blessed Assurance" song says it all.

Blessed assurance, Jesus is mine!

Oh, what a foretaste of glory divine!
Heir of salvation, purchase of God,
Born of His Spirit, washed in His Blood.

This is my story, this is my song,
Praising my Savior all the day long.
This is my story, this is my song,
Praising my Savior all the day long.

(Song was originally written by Franny Crosby, well-known blind Christian hymn writer, in 1873)

Although we're no longer the "Kids of King" (King Records is closed but still historic in Cincinnati, Ohio and still dear to our hearts), **we are now the "Kids of THE King, our Lord and Savior Jesus Christ"**! We *all* try to spread that message of peace and salvation to all that will hear, knowing that it is the way toward a positive, productive life. We still see a lot of promise in this mean, cruel, hateful world and have definitely experienced some of that first hand. But we refuse to let that negativity ever control us now. We are a unified regiment in the army of the Lord! For, God is in control for us now (always has, always will be).

Life "is one of 26 authors (… included in the) ", but I know that there is a lesson from God at the end of everything I do and I await that message regularly. I wait for God to speak to me to show me guidance, and He has always helped me to land softly. I am truly blessed for all of the angels that have crossed my path throughout my life. I'm sure that many are still always present with me and with my daughter Julia, protecting us from all of the evil and treachery that will forever be present in our world. "Angels" obviously hold a great theme for me in my life. They have helped sustain me and make me what I am today. So, I say, in conclusion, **thank you God** for having all of these "angels" (siblings, teachers, mentors, family, and friends) come my way in life, and for all those You have yet to send. They are the reason why I am still here, and why I continue on every day. Please help me be an "angel" for the next person in need.

(Please sing/play the song: "Thank You, Lord for All You've Done for Me" – by Walter Hawkins AND play "I Got That" by Anthony Brown & Group therAPy)

(To join our weekly Bible Study or to share a testimonial or comments, email me at NJKreaders21@gmail.com. Everyone stay safe out there, take care of one another, and may God forever bless you and yours.)

Naomi Joan Kinney, CPTD (Certified Professional of Talent Development) is an experienced training industry leader, writer, certified Instructional Designer, and facilitator of professional development training in various subjects across several industries (e.g., mortgage banking/finance, healthcare, retail, insurance, and higher education). Over her 30+ year training career, she has helped hospitals and many Fortune 500 organizations maintain federal, state, and local regulatory compliance. She is a published author in the subjects of Leadership Development, Diversity and Inclusion, Instructional Design, and Project Management. She included in the Association for Talent Development's (ATD's) recent publication "ATD Talent Development and Training in Healthcare Handbook". She is award-winning in her community service and in training; she is the recipient of the " 2016 CPLP Contributor Award" from the ATD's Certification Institute and holds other community honors. She is always education-focused in work and on her many volunteer projects she performs with her sorority: Delta Sigma Theta Sorority, Inc. (the Federal City Alumnae Chapter).

In college, Naomi received a scholarship to study abroad, live, and travel in Mexico extensively for five months, returning fluent in the Spanish language. Professionally, she has always involved her knowledge of the Spanish language in her training career, and after working in hospitals for many years, she eventually became a certified healthcare interpreter. She created the Interpreter Services Program at Providence Hospital DC in 2005 as their Hospital Education Director, and has held several leadership positions in the field of education and training, safety, and emergency preparedness since. She is now an Independent Training Consultant, and she continues to be a private tutor of the Spanish language on-going. Her life-long mission of educating and training others in language, cultural diversity and inclusion, and many other professional development subjects continues along with her passion for community service. She also continues to share her faith with others whenever she can. Currently, she lives in MD just outside of the nation's capital with her college student daughter and her pet beagle.

End Notes/Credits

Note: *All biblical quotations are taken from the King James version of the Bible.*

Books:

> *"On Death and Dying" – Elizabeth Kübler-Ross; Scribner, 1969.*
>
> *"Our Kind of People" - Lawrence Otis Graham; Harper-Collins Publications, 1999.*

Videos:

> *"DC on the Move" – Naomi Kinney; DC Public Access TV; 1999.*
>
> *"Spanish 101" – Naomi Kinney; DC Public Access TV; 1999.*

Songs: *(listed in the order presented in the story)*

> **"Strange Fruit"** – Billie Holliday; Commodore Records; 1939
>
> **"A Thousand Blue Bubbles"** - Johnnie Mathis; Mercury Records; 1965.
>
> **"I Got Work to Do"** - Isley Brothers; T-Neck Records; 1972.

"Sun Goddess" - *Ramsey Lewis; Columbia Records; 1974.*

"I Don't Wanna Lose Your Love" - *The Emotions; Columbia Records; 1976.*

"Mister Magic" - *Grover Washington; Kudu Records; 1975.*

"Never, Never Gonna Give You Up" - *Barry White; 20th Century Records; 1973.*

"Na Na, Hey Hey (Kiss Him) Goodbye!" - *The Steam; Fontana Records; 1969.*

"Touch Me in the Morning" - Diana Ross; Motown Records; 1973.

"You and I" - *Stevie Wonder; Motown Records; 1972.*

"It's Raining Here This Morning" - *Grandpa Jones; King Records (Shellac/Discogs); 1946.*

"Internal Love" and **"Come with Me Tonight"** – *Robert Lee Kinney, Sr. (these song names are fictitious)*

"The Eagle Stirreth Her Nest" - *Rev. Clarence LaVaughn Franklin; Joe Von Battle (Detroit record store owner and producer recorded Rev. Franklin at New Bethel Baptist Church in Detroit.); 1953.*

"Three Sheets to the Wind" - *The Willis Brothers; Star-Day Records; 1966.*

"I Guess I Better Get Up and Go Home" - *Rusty Diamond; The Lonely Sentry/Discogs; 1965.*

"Crazy Vietnam War" - *David "String Bean" Akeman; Star-Day Records; 1973.*

"Dem Bones (Gonna Rise Again)" - James Weldon Johnson (Myers Jubilee Singers); Victor Talking Machine Company; 1928.

"Born to Run" - Bruce Springsteen; Columbia Records; 1975.

"Hello, I Love You" and *"Light My Fire"* – The Doors; Elektra Records; 1968 and 1967.

"My Best Friend's Girl" and *"Just What I Needed"* – The Cars; Elektra Records; 1978 and 1978.

"Running on Empty" - Jackson Browne; Asylum Records; 1977.

"The Needle and the Damage Done" and *"Heart of Gold"* - Neil Young; Reprise Records; 1972 and 1972.

"Good Times" and *"My Forbidden Lover"* – Chic; Deluxe Records; 1979 and 1979.

"Thriller" - Michael Jackson; Epic Records; 1982.

"Purple Rain" and *"Raspberry Beret"* – Prince; Warner Brothers, Paisley Park Records; 1984 and 1985.

"Karma Chameleon" – Culture Club; Virgin Records; 1983.

"True" - Spandau Ballet; Chrysalis Records; 1983.

"Give Me the Night" and *"Love x Love"* - George Benson; Warner Brothers, Qwest Records; 1980 and 1980.

"Hot Stuff" and *"You Can't Change That"* - Raydio & Ray Parker Jr.; Arista Records; 1979 and 1979.

"Roll Bounce" - Vaughan Mason and Crew; Brunswick Records; 1979.

"Ring My Bell" - *Anita Ward; Juana Records; 1979.*

"Take Your Time" - *The S.O.S. Band; Tabu Records; 1979.*

"I'm Ready" – *Kano; Emergency Records & Filmworks; 1980.*

"O-H-I-O" - *Ohio Players; Westbound Records; 1977.*

"Drop the Bomb" - *Trouble Funk; Sugar Hill Records; 1982.*

"Bustin' Loose" - *Chuck Brown; Source Records; 1979.*

"You Give Good Love" - *Whitney Houston; Arista Records; 1984.*

"Hangin' on a String" - *Loose Ends; Virgin Records; 1985.*

"Sweetest Taboo" – *Sade; Epic Records; 1985.*

"Caravan of Love" - *Isley-Jasper-Isley; CBS Records; 1985.*

"Can You Feel the Beat?" - *Lisa Lisa & Cult Jam; Columbia Records; 1985.*

"The Power" - *Snap! (Featuring Penny Ford, who attended St. Mark with me); Ariola Arista Records; 1990.*

"Fly Away" - *Lenny Kravitz; Virgin Records; 1998.*

"Be the Change We Want to See" - *Jarrod Lawson; Dome Records; 2020;*

"Black Like Me" – *Mickey Guyton; EMI Nashville; 2020.*

"Blessed Assurance" - *Originally written by Franny Crosby; St. Augustine Records; 1873.*

"Thank You, Lord for All You've Done for Me" - *Walter Hawkins; Malaco Records; 2008.*

"I Got That" - *Anthony Brown & Group therAPy; Tyscot Records; 2018.*

Pictures:

All pictures belong to Naomi Kinney or Kinney family members.

Cover Art Work:

Cover art was originally designed by Naomi Kinney.

Map of Evanston:

Map of Evanston was originally designed by Naomi Kinney.